COMING TO JAKARTA

COMING TO JAKARTA

a poem about terror

Peter Dale Scott

M&S

Canadian Cataloguing in Publication Data

Scott, Peter Dale
  Coming to Jakarta

Poem.
ISBN 0-7710-8012-3

I. Title.

PS8587.C686C65 1988   C811'.54   C88-093240-6
PR9199.2.S268C65 1988

Set in Bembo by The Typeworks, Vancouver
Printed and bound in Canada

The publisher makes grateful acknowledgment to the
Ontario Arts Council for their financial assistance.

McClelland and Stewart
The Canadian Publishers
481 University Avenue
Toronto, Ontario M5G 2E9

For my father Frank
(1899-1985)

COMING TO JAKARTA

I.i

There are three desks in my office
        at one I read Virgil's
    descent into the underworld

at one I try to sort out
            clippings of failed Swiss banks
    or of slow killings on meat-hooks

in a well-guarded Chicago garage
            but the third desk this one
    is where the typewriter

stares at me with only
        a sheet of white paper
    from which my blank mind

is averted with an
            unmistakable almost
    diamagnetic force

as the page blurs
            to the size of a movie screen
    watched by a captive amphitheater

of all the letters there are
        containing among them every poem
    the mean vaults at the back of my head

would rather kill me than let go of
           so I turn back now
       to mock them: *Mosaic darkness*

constellations of the gulf's floor
           naked half-limbs swift
       alpine cloudburst hail and you

wind-driven ghost of snow
           down the side of the dark
       oak outside my childhood window

with the blind flapping all night
           Why are you here?
       Have you something to tell me?

I.ii

In Watertown Massachusetts
           at two in the morning
       the light Canadian novel does not help

to calm the unsteady trees outside
           that have somehow become too much
       part of my being

or the uprising in my stomach
           against so much good food and
       wine America or was it

giving one last broadcast too many
           about the Letelier assassins
       the heroin traffic

a subject I no longer hope
           to get a handle on
       and want so much to vacate

till I think of Noam
            the East Timor massacres
        he cannot publish

or was it those grim
            pre-election faces on campus
        Prepare to meet thy God

still visible under their
            freshly painted ten-foot-high
        VOTE REAGAN banners or just

tonight's vigil with Henrik and Jerry
            in the new bar off Harvard Square
        in the unused freedom of our

Halloween Nixon masks
            unable to decide between
        so many beautiful strangers

I think if I am sick now
            and cannot catch my 9:30 a.m. plane
        will I lose hold forever

of this thin bright
            thread of my particular life
        which hovers here in front

of me like an apparition
            before I get it into
        perspective leading trimly but

without forgiveness through
            the Delta departure gate?
        By its flicker I discern

the surly rebellious trees
            beyond the muttering window
        (the maples of course of my childhood

but no more full of branches
        and black openings than
    the laurels out in California)

have always concealed voices
        too low and too obscene to be heard
    except as revelations

like that face at lunch
        surging with visionary insight
    as J smiled at me

and brought his glass down
        on the marble tabletop
    too dangerously hard

or like the call from D
        with God's telephone number
    who from exhilaration

stripped for his angels
        in the Safeway parking lot
    and was held by the police

till they learned he was famous
        of course of course
    what are we if not haunted

between these temples
        this world never more full
    of immanent and transcendent glory

than when it rises up over our heads
        the future the one thing
    that cannot escape us

in front of our clumsy hands

I.iii

Taking off the
            plane tilts nearby Cape Cod
        into a map

of when I was eleven
            before it heads north safely
        above the clouds my

hand on the furtively sipped
            ginger ale can relaxes
        I look down without nausea

on the invisible peaks
            the stewardess is walking over
        as if minutes not sweaty years

separated them all Chocorua
            where I first broke out
        above a tree-line Washington

my head pounding with the fake
            clairvoyance of altitude
        Lafayette where silhouetted strangers

led us back down through
            the dense surprise blizzard
        to the festive safety

of the Dartmouth Outing Club hut
            Already we are descending
        into these shadows which

hang about as if there
            were something much more urgent
        left wholly unsaid and we

cross the supposed
            parallel which separates
        the Vermont end of Lake

Memphremagog from Owl's Head
            or Lake Massawippi my protected
        childhood summers *the true north*

The descent is bottomless
            even after I step out
        at Dorval Airport

strengthened by the sure
            pavement the one
        November snowflake on my lapel

I listen to my *un taxi*
            s'vous plêt and the
        comfort of this exotic

self unused for two decades
            relaxes or jolts me still further
        out of space into untidy

time which cannot be just
            flown over but engulfs us
        I am piloted by the Greek

immigrant taximan
            through the departed woods of
        what was once the Côte de Liesse

towards my seventy-four-year-old mother
            my father who is eighty-one
        and I am so released

as to forget tomorrow
            I will again be airborne
        losing hold seems for one moment

to be no threat
        but another beginning in
   the long voyage home

to where
we have never been

II.i

We circle and are circling
        in this planet of cloud
      on the other side of this too small

window beats the weather
        we cannot feel
      the old problem of ontological

insufficiency of having
        no answer to *Who am I?*
      no there there

yet the plane always delivers
        some illusion of landing
      scheduled soon to be the mists

of California
        the typewriter
      I am at home with

not the bare elm
        I stare through in our backyard
      as I did in the war years

towards the house of the childhood
        neighbor I would blush to meet
      after she left her blind up

but the beads of light
              on the twigs and now dancing
        water above my head did I

nearly drown once yes
              it was the summer
        Harry and I were trapped

under the rowboat
              we had tipped on purpose
        now closing us in as if

with its own animal will
              till I cannot breathe
        and suddenly to my relief

I am back on the lake
              the lake I will write about
        the complacent water

mindlessly sheening itself
              under our wharf
        where I stare down deep between the boards and see

beyond distorted caricatures of self
              green furtive shadows
        the slime of bottom weed

and among the dim stones
              the blind crawlings
        not willingly remembered

the warped plank pressing my cheekbone
              I begin to discern how
        to my relief this is to be

beyond the confines of my mind
a poem about terror

II.ii

Not that one could imagine
          at this lake and its village
      either belonging or escape

no virgin forest
          all the land private
      except when my father took me

down to the unclaimed camp
          in the pines of Black Point
      cold water slapping

the underside of the canoe
          away from the large outboards
      the still more expensive sailboats

we slip by the sagging
          mostly closed-up boathouses
      of the American estates

or rarely catch them
          with their bright awnings out
      the grass mown to the birch at the water's edge

Years later when Joan
          unlocked the door to the yellow cottage
      above Fisher's Point

entering with a candle
          because the windows were shuttered
      and the power off

as we inhaled the damp
          staining the Bartlett prints
      the mouse droppings among the blue china

it was that rare privilege
            of invading a space
        long vivid in imagination

and I think now of so many
            sinister uninhabited houses
        the white swords of glass

I had to pay for although
            I said I only went along
        with those rich American strangers

I had met on Cape Ann
            Think for yourself my mother said
        above all the unlocked screen

in the vacant Westmount mansion
            where just that once we boys
        and girls went in to play goose

the search over Aileen's
            too solid body
        as Roger whispered

outrageous urgings in my ear
            to no avail not yet
        knowledgeable enough

for that dark secret
            I went downstairs
        to play Beethoven

faster and fiercer than ever
            on the absent stranger's piano
        all of us excited

not belonging there
            we could do anything
        we never went back

never again the same gang
                yet it seems now
        natural compared to that room

adorned as I had suspected
                with an authentic nineteenth-
        century primitive landscape

long since stolen
                which we stood in front of as Joan
        told me how her ever-

absent ex-husband worked overseas
                for the CIA or perhaps
        some heavier unnamed agency

                    II.iii

What I remembered as a child
                was the green country
        all the back roads unpaved

the land once cleared
                not changing much except
        there were too many graveyards

in the fields and sugarbush
                for the number of living
        as if the stream of time

hitting the rock of Quebec
                were somehow deflected leaving
        the millpond in Moe River

where I watched my clothes
                on their willow sandbar
        go under as the sluice closed

or the drafty edifice
            in Waterville of the world's
      last snath factory

near where I rode by sleigh
            to the Compton railway station
      on the lap of the fur-coated gentleman

whose initials *L St L*
            on the gold band of his walking-stick
      next to my left eye

meant he was the local M.P.
            (brother of J.B.M.
      Saint-Laurent whose name

was painted in big green letters
            on the general store)
      going up to become Prime Minister

As I grew older I learned
            to catch when the wind was right
      the whiff of sulphite from East Angus

I read of the Magog textile strike
            the year-long fight for the diseased
      miners up in Asbestos

so much more than had met my eye
            when it barely came up to
      Mr. Lebaron's grocery counter

but it was decades after
            we rented our first house
      on the American side

from what Raleigh Elizabeth's father
            called one of the FFV
      the First Families of Virginia

and I thought it was a joke
            even when Lily's cousin
        became Secretary of State

decades after all that
            doing my eccentric research
        into the Vietnam War I

became aware of the Summer Social Register
            read in print of "Kanozas"
        "Hillside" "Bond's Adventure"

and saw for the first time
            how Lake Massawippi
        was no ordinary lake

not like Memphremagog ten miles off
            (where T.S.Eliot
        heard his celebrated *Turdus*

drip drop drip drop drop drop drop
            in Quebec County)
        but a lake where even

the names of the mailboxes
            along the American side
        were of a compact so invisible

and seamless as to exclude mere wealth
            except when duly arrived
        and so mistrustful of too high culture

as to exclude Wallace Stevens
            or Eliot himself
        yet admit those whom

I remember as
            red-faced tennis players
        slamming their angry racquets

at the Club
        It is at this moment
     rising up as if in a small plane

I see what I have to do

II.iv

I am writing this poem
        about the 1965 massacre
     of Indonesians by Indonesians

which in an article ten years later
        I could not publish
     except in Nottingham England with

a friend Malcolm Caldwell who has since
        himself been murdered   *Becker 433-36*
     no one will say by whom but I will guess

seeing as this is
        precisely poetry
     the CIA's and now Peking's Cambodian

assassins the Khmer Serai
        In that article I estimated
     a *half-million or more*

killed in this period   *P.D. Scott '75 209*
        it took Noam in a book
     suppressed by its first publisher

to quote Admiral Sudomo
        of the Indonesian junta
     more than 500,000

and now Amnesty International
        many more than one million   *Chomsky 208*
   so much for my balanced prose

But none of us experienced
        that pervasive smell of death
   those impassable rivers

clogged with corpses
        Robert Lowell is that why
   even you a pacifist

had so little to say about it?
        Or you gentle reader
   let us examine carefully

the good reasons
        you and I
   don't enjoy reading this

Like the time
        in the steep Engadine
   we saw the silent avalanche

fall away from the mountain
        hair and eyebrows
   the first to feel

the murmurations
        of the spreading
   killer wind

II.v

It takes a barbarian to recognize
        the fallibility and splendor
   of a capital

which is why you EP   *Ezra Pound*
       out of Idaho and Wyncote
    only son of an only son

at the Homeric no man's second
       when London and Paris let you down
    took as better friends

Guido and Arnaut
       dawnlight in apricot blossom
    above the massive basilica

lodged in the narrow valley
       for eight hundred years
    e lo soleils plovil   *and the sun rains*

to inhabit the past and future
       not as an evasion
    but to maintain the dialect

and as for the mirror of T'ai Tsung
       who endowed the T'ang poets and
    was felicitous in his assassins

or the fountainhead of Justinian
       whom Procopius records
    as the depopulator of Cisalpine Gaul

and whose gratuitous
       destruction of the Gothic kingdom
    opened the Po to the Lombards

what Pope Gregory
       saw not as portent but as
    fulfilment of the world's end

you had read in Dante
       trust them even as gods
    and looked for guidance to the state

so little light I cannot
            blame you who endured
        the corruption of the republic

but as for your love of splendor
            which is to say subjection
        you were too dazzled for the

muzzy language of the *damn bhuddists*
            until they put you in the wind and rain
        and Kuanon upheld you

and the leaves' tapestry
            your voice broken with authority
        As to what haunts us

the ant's forefoot
            you knew best master
        and it was hopeful your net

of fishermen's glass globes
            Kung and Eleusis
        was botched in places

wrong-headed
            so little light
        you had read the best books

and they did not save you
            it has not yet been from truth
        we have gone into war

and I was moved to reject
            the blind man's prophecy
        Odysseus

shalt lose all companions

One of those wartime summers
        I spent ten miles to the east
    in the village of Compton

with my cousin Rosemary
        haying a little
    and working in the orchards

the trees so overladen
        their limbs seemed
    to tell us by their gestures

of relief at being picked
        no men for the harvest
    that is what the war meant

to the Eastern Townships
        and otherwise
    I would not have felt

my mind simplify
        as the deepening glow
    of gold from the polished winesaps

signalled the slow approach
        of suppertime
    the good ache knotting my shoulders

and then evening
        the village of Compton
    the whole Coaticook valley

quiet as in winter
        with the roads closed by snow
    why shouldn't everyone

be able to do this
        I said then and still
     say it no matter how hard

it was later priming
        in the tobacco field
     or keeping up with the horse-drawn boat

while the girls in the shade
        sang Hungarian songs and
     racked the leaves on slats

and after this morning's
        phone call with my mother
     despite the pacifist

refugee nephew of Freud
        above North Hatley
     who asked the trespassers

not to hunt on his land
        until one of them
     came back after lunch

shot him in the back
        and the coroner of the township
     agreed it was accidental

I thought he was a bear

II.vii

It seems that where there is
        tolerance there has always been
     paranoia

I remember my own from the thirties
            when my father was away
      at so many hopeful conferences

on economic democracy
            for which the RCMP
      to my amazement

began to tap our phone
            or on peace and world order
      my first postcard from Yosemite

I could not believe there were
            such high waterfalls
      and after Canberra

a eucalyptus boomerang
            etched with cartoon koalas
      why would anyone

make our phone tick
            or write the rude editorials
      people sent my father

about the Rhodes Scholar network
            On my own I learned of
      the attacks by Joe McCarthy

and the Internal Security Subcommittee
            on professors at Harvard
      like John Fairbank

a consistent backer
            of the Chinese Communists
      or on Owen Lattimore   *'52 Hearing 3980*

among far eastern specialists
            the principal agent
      of Stalinism according to

30

his opponent in oss
        and of course on Alger Hiss
     on Leo Pasvolsky and Isaiah Bowman

the Council on Foreign Relations
        the six-man core group
     which guided the secret

War-Peace Studies
        and also drafted
     the United Nations Charter   *Shoup 153*

Years years later I then
        also reading with mistrust
     the publications of the CFR   *Council on Foreign Relations*

about oil and Southeast Asia
        when in the smallest way I found
     my father's name and Raleigh's

in the IPR Hearings   *Institute of Pacific Relations*
        no more hopeful conferences then
     and no more CCF   *Canadian socialist party*

after the advertising blitz
        in which Gladstone Murray
     the British intelligence veteran

called its leader David Lewis
        Lodz the Polish Jew
     By the time I had finished college

my father was staying at home
        once or twice he lay on the floor
     and talked to the ceiling

but mostly he was just
        getting out of politics
     I am not a swan   *F.R. Scott '86*

and he marked in his Brecht
we who desired to prepare
the soil for kindness

could not ourselves be kind   *Hamburger 321*

II.viii

At those wartime Hatley parties
         there was Lily Dulles
   the Jersey Lily

so when I went to Oxford
         I picked out her cousin
   Allen by the family name

years before a Korean bullet
         deDullicized his head
   the *New York Times*

showing the sorrowful father
         bent over the prostrate form
   of his only son   *Mosley 6*

one day before his confirmation
         as CIA director
   A decade after that

I met her niece Marian
         in San Francisco
   who knew my cousin Ibby

and held in her fashionable
         art gallery benefits
   for the Free Speech Movement

we used to dine
        in the mid-sixties
   with Marian's friends

the fast Marin set
        kids of the eastern famous
   until their marriages broke up

radicalized by day
        in the nighttime still black tie
   and then after midnight

the pool in our underwear
        it was in those
   deteriorating days that Lily

whom Marian had brought
        back into my life
   as gracious and

as talkative as ever
        told me in my car
   with its blinkers flashing

next to a hydrant
        outside her hotel
   how hard that family

had been on its sons
        Avery converted Jesuit
   son of Foster

and the untreatable Allen
        who brooded over
   his father's philandering   *Mosley 126*

his mother's therapy
        in expensive Swiss clinics
   with a disciple of Jung

And Lily told me
        of her childlessness
      it was hardest on the women

so women are fools too
        I shan't deny it
      but those relentless fathers

and I remembered
        how in front of the guests
      on the broad veranda

of a Lake Simcoe estate
        some son-in-law picked up
      the still hot squirrel

which his hound had mangled
        and blooded the face
      of his three-week-old son

or Mosley's account of Allen
        in his mother's clinic
      lashing out at his father

with *a look of absolute hatred*
        I'm never coming home
      to you ever   *Mosley 480*

II.ix

Despite my careful upbringing
        according to the handbooks
      of the post-war twenties

which urged that all family
        interactions be conducted
      in an adult rational manner

when I went back to the Rectory
         of my father's father the Archdeacon
      it pleased me to hear grace

and despite my precocious
         enlightenment about sex
      through a book about pollen and frogs

I still almost tremble
         when I think of those unexpected nights
      in the darkest corner

of my father's study
         reading his *Sexual Life of Savages*
      my introduction to the third world

with its terrifying permissiveness
         licit childhood intercourse
      customary rape

though I have since read
         how often the third world
      has just such fantasies of us

and more terrifyingly
         my introduction also
      to the quite opposite challenge

of a free modern future
         where one must throw off tabus
      This has all come back

from crouching this afternoon
         in the library stack
      with the sepia photographs

of Krause's *Bali*
         the *Marktszene* of the young pig   *Market Scene*
      muzzled and bound with raffia

its flesh clutched to the seller's
                firmly resistant breasts
        as she watches intently

the buyer's eyes free of cheating
                not the hands counting cash
        and later with the same

nostalgic crescendo
                the *Badeszene* the *Frau wäscht sich*   *Bath Scene*
        die Unterarme the *Haarwaschen*   *Woman Washing*
                                                                Her Underarms   Hairwashing
from which someone
                of that excited era
        lecher puritan aesthete or all three

has with a razor excised
                page after page in efficient
        oblongs all pairs of breasts

but not the sugary prose *so schön*   *so lovely*
                wie eine Frau   *as a woman*
        nur gedacht werden kann   *can only be imagined*

I have read elsewhere
                how this same market Bangli
        grew from nothing in the nineteenth century

when reached by international trade
                which is to say opium
        at controlled British prices

87 per cent of imports
                at Singaraja in 1859
        the rest mostly Manchester goods

until *by the end of the century*
                nearly every adult Balinese
        male and female was an addict

36

the smoke
>   *so dense in the palace*
>   *lizards fell from the walls in a stupor*   *Geertz '80 89, 204*

the terrifying power
>   of the money economy
>   Geertz could not explain

the unfavorable trade balance   *Geertz '80 202*
>   it was the old rule
>   among Chinese in Sarawak

buy for ten sell for seven
>   *pay back three*
>   *and keep four*   *May 73*

the world like myself
in its unintegrated desires

II.x

EP however nuts
>   you may have been
>   in your Wagnerian way

you were right to talk about banks
>   the problem of stored desire
>   which becomes no one's

In August 1914
>   the State Department
>   vetoed J.P. Morgan's loan to France

but the check to trade was so great
>   there was risk of depression   *Duroselle 55*
>   and with Lansing's approval

Morgan raised $500 million
        to stabilize the pound
    and restore commerce

the German response
        of unlimited submarine warfare
    and Wilson's declaration

causing gold to flow to the Federal Reserve
        $83 billion
    for the first Liberty Loan

making the U.S. Government
        the world's creditor   *Hudson 6*
    an unprecedented debt

Marian's Uncle Bill Bullitt
        on a jaunt to Moscow
    with Lincoln Steffens

for the benefit of peace   *Kaplan 245*
        A young man of great heart
    said Lenin

but *Sind sie bevollmächtigt?*
        Are you empowered?   *Kaplan 246*
    French intelligence

getting the text
        and starting a campaign
    I've never known even today

whether Wilson knew about it   *Berle 11*
        Bullitt Berle
    Isaiah Bowman all resigning

and with pain I recognize
        from my small vantage point
    in the subcommittee of four

disarmament talks
       with lights like Lodge and Moch
    so naive I wrote a memo

to ban atmospheric testing
       Why not peace now
    which Lenin has accepted?   *Bullitt 11*

Or how the Dulles clan
       sensing the historic
    foregathering at the Conference   *Mosley 57*

Allen *a little too free*
       on the Boundary Commission
    with Jules Cambon

of the Banque Paribas
       drawing a red line
    around the Sudetenland

Those were the days
       when we were full
    of a spirit of generosity   *Mosley 61*

When it was over
       it was necessary to write
    of the *wheels within wheels*

connections without coherence
       the President himself
    to say nothing of Lloyd George and Clemenceau

did not begin to know
       all that was going on
    in that cave of winds   *Baker 489; Kaplan 244*

Marian I'm sorry
       that your Uncle Bill
    a real sweetie

lived to persuade Bao Dai
        whose retinue in Hong Kong
     was paid by the Banque de l'Indochine

that he could be head of state
        with American support   *PP I 25*
     I'm sorry that Berle

so kind to my mother-in-law
        after her divorce
     lived to praise Johnson's

decision to intervene
        with U.S. troops
     and save Indonesia

from *the Chinese orbit*
        as *that of a big man*
     a towering figure   *Berle 826*

And as for the Dulles clan

II.xi

EP the year you heard Steffens
        on the lucidity of Lenin   *Stock 278*
     not yet at the end of your tether

after the German mark
        inflated a trillion-fold
     the author of the Dawes plan

to reschedule German reparations
        so that the Allies
     could continue their U.S. payments

was Lansing's young nephew
John Foster Dulles
appointed at J.P. Morgan's request   *Mosley 75*

a brilliant job
until the pyramid of debt
led to the Great Depression

Sullivan and Cromwell
handling much of the legal work
for U.S. loans in Germany

his brother Allen
at the J. Henry Schroder Bank
still closely associated

as it was in the thirties
with Schröder Gebrüder   *Marshall '81 9-11*
though Allen of course testified

his bank had no business with Nazis
in the end it was he not Foster
who saw the Nazi threat

to the global system
arranging for Sullivan and Cromwell
to leave Germany

before Dupont left the firm   *Mosley 92*
and when the partners threatened to resign
Foster capitulating   *Hoopes 47*

as Allen later told it
in tears
a rugged and rather gauche figure

with no interest in art
whose true pleasure
was sailing in rough weather

battling with elements he couldn't control　　　　　　　　　　Hoopes 41
　　　　The unequal distribution
　　of natural advantages he wrote

is one of the causes of war　　　　　　　Van Dusen 17; Dulles 58
　　　　　an international order
　　which by its very nature

is self-destructive and
　　　　a breeder of violent revolt　　　　　　Hoopes 52
　　the search for peace

through the World Council of Churches
　　　　led Foster to oppose
　　vengefulness and self-righteousness　　　　Van Dusen 94

although he would live to see
　　　　his colleague Niebuhr
　　condemn his self-righteousness

EP when counterintelligence
　　　　　threw you in a cage
　　you who had never objected

to the wealth of Barney and Cunard
　　　　drew on a compassion
　　denied to bankers and lawyers

Foster unforgiven
　　　　for opposing that war
　　and at the same time

advising Crowley
　　　　the Alien Property Custodian
　　Sullivan and Cromwell

meanwhile representing Halbach
　　　　of the I.G. Farben subsidiary　　　　　　*PM* 1/1/45
　　still controlled by Schroders

(raw materials for Hitler in London
    a powerful interest   *Time* 7/10/39
  in the victory of Franco

and an end to the proposed   *PM* 3/3/45
    nationalization of the Spanish potash industry)
  Van Dusen honors

that spiritual quest
    for *some great creative purpose*   *Van Dusen 97*
  a continuing United Nations

autonomy for subject peoples
    control of military establishments
  religious and intellectual liberty   *Van Dusen 110*

let us run with endurance
the race that is set before us

     II.xii

In the Vietnam era
    when my best friends were
  always saying *choose*

I produced footnotes on Laos
    in so-called non-
  schismogenic investigation

for my moonlight research
    which got me invited
  to an academic conference

the Concerned Asian Scholars
    in a downtown church
  opposite the San Francisco

Hilton and the AAS   *Association of Asian Studies*
            At its panel on the
    McCarthy era

history inverted itself
            Lillian Hellman and John Fairbank
    on the podium

Lattimore silent in the audience
            this fight among ourselves
    hard questions from the floor

on Fairbank's links to the SSRC   *Social Science Research Council*
            and the Ford Foundation
    after Fairbank's warning

the great danger then and now
            is politicized thinking
    either right or left

Maylie and I
            had afternoon tea
    with Wilma Fairbank

which extended towards dinner
            despite my reiterated
    warnings I had to leave

for a nighttime rally
            and TV interview against
    U.S. activities in Laos

in the darkening room
            Wilma talked of Franz Schurmann's
    abandonment of a promising

scholarly career
            for simple journalism
    one of John's best students

Heavy-hearted as I sat
            later under the
      bright klieg lights

I could think only of
            an eleven-year-old
      and four adults

canoeing among the
            waterlily pads
      of the upper Charles

hand trailing in the water
            I was allowed to taste
      their twenty-five-cent

California chianti
            as the canoes nosed
      deeper into the rushes

playing hide-and-seek
            no suggestion yet
      of the fall of the Kuomintang

the arms and narcotics traffic
            unmarked planes out of T'ainan   *P.D. Scott '72 204*
      Shig Katayama the Sumatrans   *Sampson '77 239*
                                                                           P.D. Scott '75 215

but only the inveterate
            poet and connoisseur
      Li Po

                        II.xiii

The bankers feared
            that *a German victory*
      would render gold worthless   *Blum '65 109; '70 296*

the British Treasury had been planning
to negotiate procurement
through the Chase National Bank   *Wisely 133*

I thought you were a bank
Roosevelt said
I didn't know you were a merchant   *Blum '65 101; '70 293*

None of this in Schurmann
        or William Appleman Williams
    Horowitz most eloquently silent

and in those dog days
        EP you sailed out
    through the Pillars of Heracles

to talk gold and silver
        with Unkle George Tinkham
    who needled Morgenthau

about selling British securities
        If you will pardon
    my saying so

the Secretary answered
        you are probably
    in the minority   *Blum '65 223*

Anxious to avoid
        a family quarrel with Foster
    who complained of Donovan's

crackpot *war hysteria*
        Allen maintained
    only a quiet connection

with Stephenson's New York units   *Mosley 113*
        until after Pearl Harbor
    when head of oss in Berne

he dealt with the Bank
          of International Settlements
     the first World Bank

as well as with Westrick
          his firm's Berlin representative
     and other German contacts from the twenties

for such intelligence coups
          as the Holohan mission
     which you EP

knowing less than even
          the House Armed Services Committee
     called *murder protected*   *Canto 85/559*

or Operation SUNRISE   *R.H. Smith 396; Brown 816*
          the salvaging of Italian Superpower's
     holdings in the Po Valley

on the initiative of a
          Knight of Malta
     representing his father-in-law   *R.H. Smith 114*

(with the help of McCaffery
          of Hambro's and SOE   *Special Operations Executive*
     and the Sindona affidavit)   *Lernoux 189*

and Count Volpi whose *kilowatt energy*   *Canto 80/509*
          Unkle George the isolationist
     observed *at the Lido*   *Canto 76/461*

was Italian Superpower
          and after I told Dick Smith
     the ex-CIA historian

that Allen's OSS boss
          Forgan was another director
     of Italian Superpower

his typescript came back
        with this small detail altered   R.H. Smith *116*
    into a lie indicating

someone found it significant
        perhaps because SUNRISE
    the German surrender in North Italy

led to Stalin's fury
        and Roosevelt's last assurances
    with *less than convincing candor*   Kolko *378*

Allen's Jungian mistress
        no doubt oversimplified
    when she said Allen

had come to oust the Nazis
        to make Germany *safe again*
    for the Junkers and Prussians

and of course Sullivan and Cromwell   Mosley *170*
        but when Foster and Allen agreed
    on the magic formula

to help eliminate Communism   Mosley *437*
        in Iran Guatemala
    Standard Oil and United Fruit

were not unhappy
        violence
    loving to breed violence

and then *this is something*
        that cannot be in writing
    but I prefer

a break-up of that country
furnishing a fulcrum
to help eliminate communism   *Mosley 437; P.D. Scott '85B 212*

Indonesia

II.xiv

We must consider the five sons
of Meyer Rothschild
whose clearing-houses replaced

the shipping of bullion
by a world-wide system of accounts
or what Franz Schurmann called

the most important force
for peace in the nineteenth century   *Schurmann '74 62*
and consider Meyer's grandson

Lionel First Baron Rothschild
who financed the reimbursement
of slave-owners in the dominions

and the Crimean War
a break with his anti-war policy
because the czar was an anti-Semite

The Rothschilds' worst legacy
was not that dubious boost
to the failing Ottomans of the Sublime Porte

not the flamboyance
of Gunnersbury Park
the wiles of Disraeli

not even their support
               of that clean-living young
          adventurer Cecil Rhodes

an account not reckoned up until this century
               No! it was to have invented this world
          that can only be dominated

not yet ready to govern
               Lionel who lived by
          his grandmother's confidence

War? nonsense
my boys won't let them   *Morton 90*

                    II.xv

I always thought of my father
               as a radical not like
          my grandfather who taught me grace

I was shocked years later
               when studying U.S.
          economic interests in Southeast Asia

to find he had published
               in *Foreign Affairs* the journal
          of the Council on Foreign Relations

whose name I first heard
               that brilliant afternoon
          on Raleigh's Hatley veranda

drinking what may have been champagne
               above the sailboats
          with the dark-haired Gregor

whose father it had been explained
        owned the house
    next to Eloise's by the bandstand

a second cousin of her uncle Harfie
        through the Fishes and Stuyvesants
    blood of two Secretaries of State

and was important the editor
        of *Foreign Affairs*
    and the brains as I read later

behind the War and Peace Studies
        the CFR and State project   *Shoup 119*
    Allen Dulles helped establish

the nature of their work
        precluded them from receiving
    any public remuneration or reward   *Council 24,4*

and because the memos are still secret
        we can only guess
    they proposed the creation of a CIA

Happily ignorant of all this
        I had watched Gregor
    in her white tennis outfit

how I wished I had learned tennis but
        instead I harangued her
    about German socialists

some of whom I had met
        at a six-week student seminar
    mysteriously funded

by a flurry of cold war acronyms
        I read about later
    I have since tried to imagine

describing on that veranda
        the sugary scent on a hot day
    from the corpses in Hamburg's rubble

how we who had been spared
        unlike young Harfie
    now smiling from his wheelchair

must think as survivors
        but I do not think our meeting
    could have come out otherwise

compelled largely from shyness
        to attack the column
    on an SPD sellout   *Socialist Party of Germany*

in the *Gazette*
        by her stepfather Walter Lippmann
    whose book just two years earlier

I had carefully underlined
        in the McGill library
    I challenged her head held high

beside the crabapple blossom
        with the same earnestness
    as when I underlined my calculus

the intrinsic merits of a question
are not for the public   *Lippmann 144*

II.xvi

As for banks EP
        you who wrote of Schacht
    London loans to Tibet

the decline of the Adamses
                    Sir William Wiseman who financed
          the purchase of the *Chicago News*

so that Knox could preach against
                    isolation and for war
          even if you believed

Van Buren's self-serving account
                    of how he brought down Biddle
          and the Bank in Philadelphia

to the profit of Taney's
                    banking advisers in New York
          and their correspondents the Rothschilds

a shifting of the country's financial center
                    from Chestnut Street to Wall Street   *W.B.Smith 204*
          how come in your attacks

on Roosevelt you never once mentioned
                    that chief integrator
          of Morgan policies the CFR

the Council on Foreign Relations
                    where in 1952
          it was agreed

the Guatemalan government
                    was merely carrying out the plan
          laid out for it by Oumansky

according to the study group
                    chaired by Spruille Braden
          of State and then United Fruit

Nelson Rockefeller
                    knows the situation and
          can work a little with Eisenhower on it   *Shoup 196*

the Council on Foreign Relations
          for whom William Henderson of Mobil
     called Southeast Asia

vitally significant an
          economic and strategic prize   *Shoup 227*
     in those dog-day fifties

when I more suited
          than any bank clerk
     felt honored to meet Dean Rusk

thought Sastroamidjojo boring
          and mimicked the trembling hands
     of Penn Nouth who sat beside me

in the C's of the United Nations
          and whose friends are now all dead
     Henderson called for an *interventionist*

unlimited final commitment   *P.D. Scott '74 127*
          or in the words
     of the CFR-commissioned study

by Russell H. Fifield
          sometime State Department official
     professor of political science

at the University of Michigan
          and the National War College
     Secretary of the Association

of Asian Studies
          a challenge of major proportions   *Fifield 3*
     in which the CIA's clients

who had just been defeated
          in the '58 Sumatra revolt
     could not *be overlooked*

in Indonesia's future
        if only because   P.D. Scott '75 219
    of their rare qualities of leadership   Fifield 312

II.xvii

Training and education for leadership
        can be an important
        indirect result

of the U.S. military program   Fifield 102
        wrote Fifield who must have known
    what Ford and the University

of California were up to
        officer corps disciplined
        eager to get things done

anti-Communist in outlook
        attributes of leadership
        not widely found

in Southeast Asia   Fifield 300
        such was the academic
    language of Professor Fifield

not in any indictable sense
        a war criminal
    nor I suppose Guy Pauker

another of those jet-lagged
        CFR policy consultants
    a displaced Rumanian

so deferential
        about his quite adequate English
    when we debated Vietnam

before the pitiless Irvine students
            and while on the
        RAND payroll the founder

of an academic center at Berkeley
                where as professor of political science
            he developed the program

to train the cadres of
        SESKOAD the Indonesian
    army command school

of which I knew nothing
                when confused
        by a sudden surge

of my old combativeness
                saying *you*
        political scientists

are part of the problem
                and the students all
        starting to applaud I

hushed them and turned
                to apologize *of course*
        not you personally

I did not know then
                you had publicly castigated
        old friends in

the Indonesian military
                for not *carrying out*
        a control function

for lacking
                the ruthlessness
        that made it possible

for the Nazis to suppress
the Communist Party
a few weeks after the elections

in which the Communist Party   P.D. Scott '75 231
won five million votes   *Pauker '64 221-23*

II.xviii

I was always going along
             at first with whatever
sounded most reasonable

and that is why
             in the late fifties
I would have agreed with John Fairbank

attacked for his love of China
             that to have got $30 million
through the Social Sciences Research Council

from John Brigham Howard
             international research and training
director of the Ford Foundation

for academic studies of China
             would be *an important means*
for bringing it that is to say the

cold war *to an end*   *Fairbank 111*
             and why in the seventies
I agreed with the CCAS

the Committee of Concerned Asian Scholars
             on the need to investigate
the considerable correspondence

between the aims of the research committee
          set up by John Fairbank
and what General Dick called

research needs in the social sciences
          relevant to the U.S. Army's
          limited war needs   *Bulletin 92-93*

yet now in the eighties
          this dispute among friends
who might with a little reflection

have understood each other
          seems less important
than the discovery it was the Ford

Foundation with MIT
          which first sent Guy Pauker
to Indonesia and then

$2.5 million to Pauker's students
          for training the officers at SESKOAD
In the words of John Brigham Howard

whom one learns from *Who's Who*
          was formerly depchief
of AMAG in Greece   *American Military*
                                           Advisory Group

millions in military aid
          to what even the Twentieth
Century Fund called rightist terror

Ford felt it was training the guys
          who would be leading the country
which is to say Indonesia

when Sukarno got out   *Ransom 99; P.D. Scott '75 233*
          and the Ford man in Jakarta
Michael Harris the former

labor rep in Paris
>> when the CIA passed millions
>> to split the French labor movement

was said by one member
>> of the UC Indonesia project
>> *to have felt himself superior*

to the U.S. Ambassador   *P.D. Scott '85B 216-17*
>> in his work with the CIA
>> the Asia Foundation

and those whom at first
>> I declined to mention   *P.D. Scott '75 255*
>> *(in our sort of life*

people of sound mind
>> *had to shut their eyes)*   *Mandelstam 58*
>> whom Pauker called

at the Nugan Hand meeting
>> *the so-called Berkeley Mafia*
>> *I talked them into coming*

to the University
>> *running the country today*
>> *fun to have around*   *Kwitny 310*

with devastating consequences   *Mandelstam 58*

III.i

According to the court poets
　　　　of the *Babad Tanah Jawi*
　　　Agung could have destroyed Batavia

by his occult power
　　　　he had his commander Purbaya
　　　fly through the air

to make a hole in the wall
　　　　with a thaumaturgical utterance
　　　and his commander Madureja

whom he knew to be a traitor
　　　　give fight with his troops
　　　until all were slain

so that the grateful Dutch
　　　　sent envoys to Mataram
　　　with annual tribute

estimated by Vlekke
　　　　at 60,000 guilders
　　　in the most expensive year

in exchange for which
　　　　the sultan Agung
　　　forced the coastal people

to deliver rice and wood
　　　　at no cost to himself
　　　in forty-one years the company

made a profit of 25 million guilders
　　　　of which 9.7 million
　　　were remitted to Amsterdam   *May 15-16*

This is how it was
            before the World Bank
Royal Dutch Shell

the destruction of the rain forests
            8000 species a year
power and submission

There have always been poets

III.ii

To have learnt from terror
            to see oneself
as part of the enemy

can be a reassurance
            whatever it is
arises within us

fear
            a matter of self-protection
quick wits in the urban streets

where my parents for socialist reasons
            lived in the thirties
and my toys reluctantly shared

seemed always to disappear
            except when I was conducted
to play alone on the lawn

of the nearby campus
            or dressed up in polished
gaiters with a buttonhook

to go have tea with Gran
            or Christopher and his maiden aunts
        at the edge of Mount Royal

there were in our house
            so many meetings
        but when my parents hugged

I would get between their knees
            to be *in the carriage*
        I used to be sent out

to play in the snow till lunch
            or until the pack
        of boys took my sled

I recall much blood
            the time I hit Babs
        whom I remember as so gentle

or the broken window
            as black as the lake's bottom
        after I had been chased

one more time behind
            our insecure board fence
        and in response to the rain

of catcalls and heavy gravel
            I needing to kill someone
        heaved a primeval rock

high across the back lane
            and into the very nest
        of the office typewriter

in the flat of Professor Sullivan
            who in the post-war years
        when he taught me calculus

amused the whole class
                by retelling the tale
        after all it was not he

who had to bear
                the lasting damage
        of that jangling chord from the struck

keys I could never
                replicate on this machine
        What I am talking about

I lack
                therefore I am
        however childish and

imperfectly remembered
                is ontological
        has to do with the rare times

one trembles in bed
                from terror
        out of love

one will completely dissolve
                into this other person
        or when looking for encouragement

to the familiar
                repetitions of the stars
        one recognizes

whatever that noble movement
                you and I are not designed
        for this world we now live in

III.iii

Still less that first lake
        my grandfather's near Ste. Agathe
    so primeval it had no name

no road to the clearing
        and tree-trunk we used as a dock
    where Elizabeth and I

used to run naked
        among the spruce stumps
    or wade in the deep ooze

among the water lilies
        and murderous pitcher plants
    on the rotting logs

which ringed the lake
        bubbles of methane
    from soft things under our toes

We washed in water from a rain-barrel
        at a corner of the cabin
    pitched among boulders

where M. Desjardins
        watched his Guernseys even
    plowed a few desperate furrows

None of us belonged there
        not even the white horse
    we could not find the site of the farmhouse

when I went back with Selma
        snuck up the back way
    through Anson McKim's

and after a few hours
        the first rainstorm of that summer
    extinguished our hissing fire

my hopes of belonging
        to the pre-Cambrian north
    No! If I am to use language

then Lake Massawippi
        the one lake
    I could come back to

is the one we must deal with

III.iv

A poem of water
        why not the mountains
    the freedom on summits

to come down any side
        even the familiar one
    these afternoons I

walk up past the Rad Lab
        to look west from Grizzly Peak
    above the dim mists

in the skyscrapers
        the boats going nowhere
    and with dusk the first urgent

flashes of the signal
        taking over the night
    from uninhabited Alcatraz

just as when we had moved
            partly for my sake
    to Westmount Mountain

to go to school with kids
            who unaffectedly
    bore the names of firms

Birks Jewellers or Frosst's
            Neo-Chemical Food
    while the neighbor we never knew

except from the newspapers
            owned the Timmins gold mine
    yes then I felt liberated

looking out from Summit Circle
            where there were no fights
    over the city spread like a map

the Sun Life Building in the fog
            the dull murmur of the rapids
    the grainboats frozen in the canal

Under my mother's paintings
            and my father's piano
    I looked alone through the encyclopaedia

checking our family tree
            which my father pulled
    from a dusky trunk behind the furnace

futilely against the dukes
            and earls listed by name
    and date and little else

and in the warmth of spring
            I would go out before breakfast
    to look for the first bloodroots

in the park across the street
            or later that once
      our own white bodies

or just to play baseball
            with these children I called friends
      and when the black taxi

passed us and then stopped
            its passenger lay down in the street
      the soles of his shoes sticking up

and someone put a sheet
            over the rest of him
      I looked for it in the newspaper

and there were I believe instead
            the first headlines in my memory
      CHAMBERLAIN FLIES TO MUNICH

and the PEACE IN OUR TIME
            for which I woke up my parents
      to my embarrassment

I am losing the thread
            but yes it was that winter
      I sat up all night

by the window I was not supposed to close
            to face off the ghost of snow
      on the side of the oak tree

coming down as it seemed
            straight into my bedroom
      and could not turn away

or go back to the head of my bed
            until it faded in the dawn
      I still go to the high mountains

that rush of safe giddiness
        when I stand up and look around
    at so much visibility

flight
        immersion
      No! If we are to escape

we must go another way

III.v

That bright island of non-being
        when I was eleven
    in Cambridge Massachusetts

as much of an escape
        into an exotic civilization
    as were those summers

near Ste. Agathe to something
        else I never was
    playing for the first time

with other sons of professors
        the son of a World Court judge
    the poet George Barker

as he was coming downstairs
        drinking the orange juice
    off my father's breakfast tray

and it was too much for our maid Georgette
        left speechless hands stretched
    across the alcove

transported too far
          from her native village in the Beauce
     Je suis la croix blanche   *I am the white cross*

vous m'avez rempli   *you have filled me*
          de forces électriques but I   *with electric current*
     for myself was glad to have

arrived among children who did not
          drag each other fully clothed
     into the gym shower glad

to trade Willkie buttons and debate
          in our small absolute way
     the need to get into the war

as Canada already had and whether
          I too should sing in the chorale
     the words about *bad King George*

glad not to be the first
          to be rebuked by Miss Thorp
     the great-niece of Longfellow

for being too rambunctious
          after school though next year
     I was less fit than before

to survive Westmount
          Junior High School among
     the draft dodgers who jammed Donald

from the Weirdale Orphanage
          accused of stealing pencils
     into the classroom waste-paper basket

such an easy mark that soon
          he quit school joined the Navy
     and was blown up by a sub in the St. Lawrence

I have to say that I myself once started
                that weekly joke *It's Donald's birthday*
        as if that might deflect the storm

Those years I mostly waited for the summers
                yet even now in North Hatley
        back among the Americans

I was either too snobbish or too uncouth
                either from uncompetitiveness
        or natural contrariety of mind

for that long season of
                canoeing and freestyle races
        the parents lined up on the dock at the Club

drinks in their hands and cheering
                Surely there must be
        some other way to grow up

I used to think with the water
                of the winners' kicks in my face
        or at the hour

of the confident male laughter
                from the six p.m. sherry parties
        I would rather listen to

from far up
                in the silent beech forest
        where I had gone back sullenly

to look for lady's slippers
                and found once deep in leaves
        three blue and brown speckled eggs

of what must have been
an ovenbird's nest

III.vi

Soon I would sail away
        through the ice storms of the North Atlantic
    as if to be born

with the leather briefcase
        I would use for a quarter century
    Betty Ann gave me the day

I said to her *thank you*
        and now good-bye
    after two righteous years

of the McGill Choral Society
        of McGill Outing Club hikes
    with their roughly innocent overnights

and of rallies of support
        against police brutality
    having seen

the glint of horses' hooves
        in the dark foreign-speaking crowds
    on the sidewalks of St. Lawrence Main

the pushing so determined
        on both sides of the Iron Curtain
    to establish the post-war era

with so much intrigue
        the result was complicity
    as in a small way

even I discovered
        the night five of us
    two friends one fellow-traveller one CP   *Communist Party*

roneoed the leaflets   *mimeoed*
            for an illegal march
        against the ban on marches

sworn to secrecy that night
            a blinding five a.m. rain
        we never handed the leaflets out

but the police came anyway
            first plain-clothes and then Mounties
        finally drawing a big crowd

enough for page three of the *Gazette*
            there being more than meets the eye
        to the politics of reason

and I do not know to this day
            whether one of us was an informant
        and whether even he

knew which side
            he was really working for
        nor to what extent

his wishes
could be distinguished from my own

                    III.vii

I arrived in no mood
            for the obligatory pluralism
        of post-war Oxford

where in our seminar
            on *Recent European
        Political Thought*

we were persuaded to read three dons
                from the south side of Broad Street
        and three from the north

my suggestion of Sartre
                meeting with a look which convinced
        even me I had just been joking

But where the theatrics of the gown
                turned Wordsworth back
        on his inner tranquility

they left me self-conscious
                the more insecure
        alone on Snowdon —

straddling a hog's back
                my giddiness
        in the dense fog

like a rodeo rider
                but in the end the sunburst
        over the summit revealed

no more than a cog railway
                sloping down into the west
        Then I discovered Hegel

sweet dialectics — now I knew
                the *world* was *an sich*
        and *I* was *für sich* the

no reality without accident
                which so annoyed the famous don
        if Hegel wrote that he shouldn't have

and even my kindly
                All Souls tutor
        whom I did not know

had himself been ploughed   *Berlin 118; failed*
            said of my mock-writtens
        they'll think you're insane

that was it — when Sally
            who had surprised me with a kiss
        on the canal towpath

outside Long Wittenham
            came to my digs for tea
        I tripped over the electric fire

branding the Astrakhan carpet
            of Mrs. Foxley-Norris
        and the only solution

stared up at me
            out of the mystic
        cipher at my feet

I was going mad
            the world even the war
        in Korea forgotten

for the momentary solace
            of incapacity
        body and fingers stretched

and I hear again my voice
            failing to reach me
        remember the long search

under moaning walnut-trees
            in the night rain near Limoges
        high wind off the Atlantic

to find any shelter
            one leg over the high
        courtyard wall when suddenly

the mastiff leapt up
            to the limit of its chain
        no sleep after that

and the next afternoon
            over the Puy-de-Sancy
        blocked by new snow from arriving

for Easter mass in the remote
            church of Orcival
        I swear I see

beyond the humming phone wire
            and glistening black asphalt
        a face in the heavy clouds

or was it
            in the strange light
        an intimation

of those shapes in the brooding
            toils of energy
        and deluge of emotion

we all carry within us

III.viii

As predicted the famous don
            frustratingly sympathetic
        said *but your Hegel questions*

sounded almost like Michael Foster
            and I thought back
        to the tea and crumpets

in the ill-lit immense
        study at Christ Church
    with the one don I found

not just a friend but in some ways
        a holy man as if
    in the wrong place and age

so there was no extra year
        as editor of the *Isis*
    it was back to Canada

and a small school
        for the over-privileged
    in the woods of the Seignory Club

where at night I read
        about Yvain in the forest
    com hon forsenez et sauvage   *like a man frantic and wild*
                                                              Yvain 2838

but after the weekly movies
        the whole school cheering
    the gooks on Okinawa

once more incinerated
        in the jets of napalm spewed
    from the tanks of the Marines

lights out the generator switched off
        I would go out in the moonlight
    boots squeaking on snow

to empty the steadily filling
        buckets of maple sap
    into the boys' vats

and stoke their banked fires
        the woods' shadows numinous
    with sugary smoke

and I have since believed
in the face of
every nuclear headline

the force flooding those
millions of high trees
even in the frost of night

will survive the next war
whether or not we do
and I found I had the courage

to make my young warriors
read one account
of an actual lynching

jabbering foaming at the mouth
horrible white of his eyes   *Davies 141*
till they begged me to stop

to say it didn't happen
now that was a discovery
Three years later I went back

on my honeymoon with Maylie
to that tall carpeted room
over Christ Church Meadow

asking in effect
from this same new-found power
How can you stand it here?

And Michael Foster a few months
before he shot himself
looked around at the oak

panels from Cardinal Wolsey
and said *I can't imagine*
any better life

III.ix

With the same remoteness
        or if you will emancipation
    by which I managed

to be ploughed at Oxford   *failed*
        I went on for three years
    without falling in love

and for what then seemed tragic
        I can have no regrets
    there is something to be said

for being marginal
        and even insular
    at the vortices of culture

like Oxford and Harvard
        where the sons of the wealthy
    at their Eliot House breakfasts

ate only the yolks of their eggs
        Certainly I was glad
    to have been drafted neither

for Kenya nor Korea
        neither the black-tie dinners
    of my Rhodes Scholar roommates

nor the emphatic
        intellectual summitry
    of the Harvard Junior Fellows

all chosen for high careers
        If we were large-minded enough
    and could plough everyone

send them back to the forests
            like Yvain or Erlangga
            like the heroes of all good tales

then no one would have
            needed to look shocked
            that night in New York

when in the company of
            my friends the Rhodes Scholars
            and Junior Fellows

gearing up to publish
            their policy dissertations
            to burst upon the world

of think-tanks the CFR
            and consulting for agencies
            as yet unnamed

I said *That's why*
            some people in Europe
            are not so upset

to see Russia get the bomb
            and you could hear the drinks
            of the future ambassadors

being set down

III.x

The stream one lives by
            one hardly hears
            we are not astronauts

who see today's light
        as a disc of radiance
    inhabiting darkness

and to that reader
        who like myself has been plunged
    to the heart of once terrifying

now daily love
        it will be clear why these words
    cast no dark shadows

though there was once such a dawn
        the word *love* itself decays
    till it loses meaning

and now that to think
        of escape is meaningless
    and one feels free

even to scream rather than escape
        indeed could one ever scream
    this way at God I wonder

how exonerate her
        for the criminal defects
    of the whole establishment

including life itself
        she first delivered me from
    unlike everyone else

even my dear father and mother
        whose saving dissatisfactions
    I look back on as defined

even my own children
        issuing forward
    like the new energy

spilling from clefts in the ocean bed
        you will not see her
    anywhere in this poem

except as one sees light
        as in the darkness
    floating between my thigh

and my quiet fingers
        she may seem no more than a
    rest within space

no more than a
        pivot
    for the restless movements of the stars

she being within the
        crannies of what is written
    beyond what it limits

and when she sleeps

III.xi

After my father's biographer
        has visited I have
    this dream of sitting

beside the door of our house
        from which bodies are being
    removed it becomes

more and more clear there is
        some kind of major scandal
    though the house is mine now

I am not aware of
            terror even guilt
        it is more like the discovery

of Philip of Macedon's tomb
            in museum photographs
        the tunnel having been dug

through generations of suppressed
            memory by the biographer
        how my great-great-grandfather

John Scott came to Montreal
            on one of the cholera ships
        to open a stationery shop

and died soon after
            as did his eldest son
        leaving young William Edward

to support the whole family
            as apothecary's apprentice
        and eventually doctor

five of whose nine children
            died by the age of four
        of the family consumption   *Djwa 14-15*

my grandfather Frederick George
            the first not suckled
        by his mother and also

the first to survive — a poet
            and young Anglo-Catholic curate
        who drawn to a monastery

when his sister parents
            and beloved died
        wrote *when Death comes*

Sin sits and hums
          A chaunt of fears
     my grandfather the jovial

Beloved Padre who walked
          into No Man's Land
     on all sides the brown mud   F.G. Scott 156-57

and desolate mist till he saw
          the hand of my Uncle Harry
     with the Scott family ring   *Djwa 38*

the bloodstone fake crest I wear myself
          on the little finger
     Uncle Arthur too the prize-winning

debater in high school
          who never spoke again in public
     I could feel my legs paralyzed

as if turning to stone
          and became a notary
     and yet my father the thirties pacifist

his four older brothers
          all dead or badly wounded
     was only prevented from enlisting

at seventeen by the rifle
          which exploded in his hands
     and blew out one eye

life after that
          so concentrated in his tingling limbs
     he became like his own father

poet reformer domestic tyrant
          the father whom as a child
     he had avoided sick in bed

84

I see my father in the dying man
       and straight toward me
   endless the known and unknown roadways run   F.R. Scott 169

it is all coming out
       the funeral I must have forgotten
   Dick Scott

torpedoed in the St. Lawrence
       I have not escaped death's nudge
   they are emerging now

from the house of my dream
       the dead
   and the survivors

the fallen apples of the dead
       beyond ourselves
   the yet untasted

tree of life

                    III.xii

After the ritual
       procession to the sea
   and the empty beach with its spirits

a cockfight much feasting   *Belo 99*
       the shadows gather
   of the village ancestors

in the *wajang koelit*
       the shadow play
   adapted to centuries

of invading powers
                now no more than fragments
        of the original story

the Barata Yudda or great war
                delighting its audience
        less with its five heroes

the virtuous Pendawas
                of Hindu origin
        aloof esoteric Arjuna

the too *perfectly just*   Geertz '73 139
                banished to the forest
        than with the heroes' servants

the clown Toealen
                true Indonesian ancestor
        black pot-bellied

permanently pregnant   de Zoete 156
                who by his crafty
        knowledge of the occult

makes his hero appear
                always to be conqueror   Covarrubias 241
        or the clown Semar

Falstaffian jester
                who when the too dutiful
        Arjuna under orders

comes to execute him
                replies *old friend*
        I will burn myself

in the fire rising
                to defeat Shiva
        so the war starts again   Geertz '73 139-40

Visitors cannot understand
        how the great crowds
        can go on watching till dawn

or in the case
        of the *tjalonarang*
        the powerful exorcism

how after a day's work
        the village dancers
        go so easily into trance

to *bring the gods down*
        not that this will
        have anything to do with

the rising birth rate
        or the shortage of land
        but the anger they rarely show

fires the combat
        between the terrible witch Rangda
        her long hanging breasts

realistically made
        of bags of white cloth
        filled with sawdust   *Covarrubias 326*

not only a fear-inspiring figure
        she is Fear
        afraid as well as frightening   *Bateson and Mead 35-36*

whose deathly plague has
        destroyed the kingdom
        of her son Erlangga

and the good dragon Barong
        whose sheepdog coat
        glitters with mica

moving among the kris dancers
        entranced by Rangda
    to return them to consciousness

gentle Balinese father
        according to Bateson and Mead
    a frenzied trancer

has only to rub his face
        in the Dragon's beard
    to be calmed   *Bateson and Mead 38*

even Rangda who may run amok
        headlong into the *gamelan*   *orchestra*
    or be deranged for weeks

has her comic moments
        as when she pretends to polish
    the mirrors on Barong's coat

while members of the crowd
        in trance around the courtyard
    rush out to stab themselves

wrestle with one another
        devour live chicks or excrement
    as the spectators

relieve them of their krisses
        because those not fully
    estranged can wound themselves

until towards dawn
        the actor possessed
    by the real Rangda

is brought with effort under control
        one old actor is said
    never to have regained

his mental balance   *Covarrubias 331*
        and the great battle is
    once more a standoff

III.xiii

It was after I looked up
     , C.F. Adams of Pan Am
because of Air America and

the CIA's phony Laos crisis
        of 1959   *P.D. Scott '72 10-15*
    that I found out I knew

not one but two Adamses
        Gill the sophomore
    who dropped out of Radcliffe

to live in the Berkshires
        singing madrigals
    and whose father (through

Paul Mellon's Bollingen Foundation)
        published the books
    I was then reading

by Curtius and Auerbach
        on imperial pastorals
    parola ornata   *Curtius 71, 357*

ascent from the depths   *Curtius 6*
        and forest romances
    commissioned by the wives

of absent crusaders
        dir soave e piana   *Auerbach 66*
    which even if Europe

should now lose its power
> *has prefigured a common life* Auerbach 338
and the other Adams

George Homans president
> of the American Sociological Association
who went so quickly down the lake

to fetch my father
> from the camp on Black Point
when Maylie went into hospital

and who wrote about rank
> *If his behavior had improved*
> *his social rank might then have risen* Homans '50 180

no one had more verve
> for those Hatley cocktails
but when my cousin Ibby

protested the napalmed
> villages in Vietnam
George shouted at the surprised

Canadians *we will win*
> *we will win*
George is it possible

I wonder speaking myself
> as a refugee third-
generation Canadian poet

that we are all victims
> of excessive inheritance
after all you yourself

apparently believed
> *every single bit*
> *of human behavior*

III.xiv

My mother walked out of that
            Hatley get-together
        I never had the guts

to walk out of the
            quadripartite
        disarmament talks at the UN

while Henry Cabot Lodge
            in his impeccable
        Champs Elysées café French

was putting on another of his
            affected or possibly sincere
        stupidity acts

thus forestalling
            what was probably in any case
        the quite imaginary risk

of disarmament I
            am not suggesting
        Valerian Zorin was any different

still less that the problem was
            automatically one of caste
        Kent School's Jake Beam

having learnt to speak Polish
            to President Zawadzki
        the former railway worker

with a good humor that
        disqualified him
     for the hard-edged nightmare

at the power center alas
        so many new nations
     so many ambitious men

still candidates for
        the curse of pre-eminence
     not yet terrorized by war

and now bloodbaths in peacetime
        they have designed for themselves
     with the insomniac clarity

one associates with mountains
        the roof of the world
     the long faces

in D.L.1   *Defense Liaison 1 (External Affairs)*
        when they heard the new Prime Minister
     had signed without thinking

the NORAD agreement
        slipped him as if routine   *Ignatieff 188-89*
     or even that private UN dinner

out on Long Island the
        Iranian host a Cypriot
     the Ethiopian princess whose uncle

died later in the coup
        and when my boss called me back
     for the meaningless midnight

vote in the UN First Committee
        it was mountain clear
     driving in on the freeway

at sixty miles an hour
        my life entrusted willingly
    to the unpromising

strangers on my right and left
        that the government of the world
    could be arranged like this

the problem not so much
        simple human incompetence
    or evil on all sides

but those unique degradations
        which follow upon any
    categorical assumption

of command

III.xv

The year
        I was consul in Warsaw
    hour after morning hour

I would tell the marriageable
        village princesses
    fatally decked out in their best

hand–embroidered *strój*   *folk dresses*
        who had risen at 2:30 a.m.
    to catch the milk train

that if they too
        wished to visit cousins
    in the mining towns

of flat northern Ontario
            for a six-week holiday
        then unlike their post-

menopausal mothers and aunts
            they would have to get x-rays
        and apply through Ottawa to become

landed immigrants I having taken
            only seconds to size up
        their nubility

and then deliver
            the disastrous verdict
        to certain tears and pleadings

which in turn came back
            in not necessarily unpleasant
        ways to haunt my dreams

No one should have to or be
            allowed to last in such a job
        the talent for power

being almost certainly
            a disqualification
        just as governments

that limit themselves
            with domestic restraints
        Athens Rome England even Spain

almost immediately
            in an unfilled world
        explode into empires   *Marshall '87 227*

like giant doomed stars

III.xvi

Strictly speaking
            the only multinational financier
            I ever knew was Raleigh

youngest child
            and gentlest father
            and if I remember him

once wearing a cutaway
            it was only as a joke
            on himself at a Halloween party

or perhaps when I was seven
            and married his daughter Elizabeth
            in a Lachute barn

no Marxist could have talked with Raleigh
            for one hour and still hated him
            and yet it was Raleigh

in his unsung job
            with an insignificant pension
            in the investment department

of the Sun Life Assurance Company
            Montreal's largest
            who dealt with Curtis Calder

of Havana Electric
            Shanghai Power Company
            and Italian Superpower

Raleigh who when we had tea
            in his small retirement apartment
            to talk about finance

had never heard
of Meyer Lansky's racetrack
leased to him by Citibank

where he corrupted
the Cuban politicians or
of Tu Yueh-Sheng's Green Gang

which Chiang and Tai Li
used to wipe out the Shanghai
Communists and run the dope traffic

Raleigh and his department
who innocently
as the Aswan engineers

not thinking about snails
helped persuade
a reluctant General Motors

to build a plant in South Africa
so that the earnings
from Sun Life's premiums

could be invested in place
and not create pressure
on the Krugerrand

In accordance with Plato
he kept to his station
as the best of us have done

III.xvii

The Radja had expected
his palace to be attacked
from the south side

as martial custom would require
            but unexpectedly
        the Dutch made for the north

his household
            in a collective frenzy
        half dazed with opium   *Geertz '80 11*

set the palace on fire
            all his relatives
        dressed in their white finest

with gold ceremonial krisses
            the women even more
        enthusiastic than the men

in short white loincloths
            covered with jewelry
        their hair loose

carrying spears broken in half
            to be used at close range
        The procession left the palace

with the Radja at its head
            on a man's shoulders and protected
        by his gold umbrellas of state

entranced women and boys
            marched up the avenue
        to the astonished Dutch

who gave orders to halt
            but they only walked faster
        then made an insane rush

the soldiers fired the first volley
            and a few fell but
        the frenzied men and women

continued to attack
            the soldiers to avoid
        being overrun were obliged

to fire continually
            someone with a kris
        went around killing the wounded

he was shot down but
            an old woman took the kris
        and continued the bloody task

the wives of the Radja
            stabbed themselves
        in a heap over his body

when the horrified soldiers
            stopped firing
        the women threw gold coins

yelling that it was payment
            for a final shot
        or else stabbed themselves

everywhere broken spears
            krisses with gold handles
        studded with diamonds and rubies

in pools of blood   *Covarrubias 34-35*

A woman survivor
            who fainted when cut
        by the spear of a falling man

told Covarrubias
            all she remembered was
        the cool hissing of the bullets

like music

IV.i

Mégève   coming down
                beside a rainbow
        into a shower

glissade 1000 meters
                on wet grass
        laughter at falling safe

think   married a Venezuelan
                and lives near Lausanne
        tell me now you

with homes in the mountains
                who are at hand
        and know all things

where we hear only rumor
                of the captains
        at Bilderberg meetings

one has to sound
                like a John Bircher to talk about
        between the Rockefellers

the Agnellis and the Rothschilds
                at whose Mégève resort
        we were lodged in uncomfortable

luxury as delegates
                to the International Student Service
        Bilderberg meetings

supplying Prince Bernhard with
                an almost unrivalled network   *Doyle 20*
        not just for the European Movement

financed with German counterpart funds
        but also for the recruitment
    of old intelligence contacts

as conduits for Lockheed payoffs
        through the Temperate Zone
    Research Foundation

for Antelope Cobbler the Italian premier   *Sampson '77 135-36*
        which supplemented the CIA's
    financial support

to parties candidates
        and incumbent leaders
    of almost every political persuasion   *Church I,146*

and under Sukarno
        which is why I am telling all this —
    not just recalling

the swampy fields
        around the Rockefeller lodge
    in the Connecticut valley

where the Liberty Lobby discovered
        the Bilderbergers in '67 —
    Jakarta payments deflected

four months before the coup   *Sampson '77 184-85*
        at legal risks to Lockheed   *'76 Hearings 962*
    towards the *very wealthy*

General Alamsjah
        epitome of
    the military entrepreneur   *Crouch 243*

whom a Lockheed memo
        called *the second man*
    the coup made at once

funds available to Suharto   *'76 Hearings 962*
     a Lockheed web   *P.D. Scott '85A 256*
     extending from Geneva to Jakarta   *Sampson '77 120*

millions to Japanese officials
     where *every move made*
     was approved by Washington   *Sampson '77 228*

the money through Deak
     back to Shig Katayama
     in the Cayman Islands   *'75 Hearing 909*

the Wildlife Fund the Sultan
     Castle Bank in the Bahamas
     Helliwell narcotics CIA   *Kruger 15-16*

the name Richard M. Nixon on the list   *'75 Hearing 241*
     It was at a Bilderberg
     meeting that Prince Bernhard

was introduced by Baron
     Edmond de Rothschild
     to Tibor Rosenbaum of the ICB   *Doyle 20*

the International Credit Bank   *Naylor 22*
     (later exposed by the Baron
     after the Vesco coup

as *a source of secret funds*
     for the Mossad
     Israel's intelligence service

and one of the country's primary
     weapons brokers)   *Hougan 172*
     and whose colleague Ed Levinson

was the power behind
     the Havana Riviera   *Reid 226*
     and the Serv-U Corporation

of the Bobby Baker payoffs
        which began to be exposed
    in November 1963 —

My book would have asked
        as the Warren Commission staff
    working for Allen Dulles

was unable to
        why Levinson's pit-boss
    McWillie *gambler and murderer*   *23 WH 166*

from the old Binion gang
        in Dallas and Fort Worth
    who *had a fix with Mr. Big*

I don't think we'd better
        go into that phase of it   *Reid 156-57*
    twice brought to Havana

most likely as a courier   *AR 152*
        his close friend
    Jack Ruby

A dumb subject
        The book went into galleys
    and was photographed

for the Pocket Books spring catalogue
        but never published
    freeing me

to write this poem
        Do you remember   yes
    just for an instant

the sun warm on our shoulders
                and beyond the mists
        rising from the meadow

Mont Blanc

                    IV.ii

From the Bay Bridge
                on the way home from the opera
        you could look down on the searchlights

of the Oakland Army Terminal
                where they loaded the containers
        of pellet-bombs and napalm

into black Japanese ships
                over which the cranes
        bent like anxious surgeons

in the calm and glassy night
                People of good will
        of whom at first there were many

were willing to sign petitions   *Powers 36*
                or to help in drafting
        the letter to the *Times*

about how in six months
                they had moved from true to false
        reports of the North Vietnamese

negotiating position   *Schurmann '66 92-93*
                that letter never published
        and the music changing

bonfires to still the streets
> the first smudges of tear gas
> the Yellow Submarine

(acid in Big Sur
> Allen kneeling to pray
> for Johnson's health)

at the rock poetry festival
> no sensations from my first joint
> except for the difference

between the salt and pepper
> I felt being shaken
> on my bare left arm

Owsley by parachute
> at the Human Be-in
> Mika on Carole's shoulders

on mine so they could see
> *the Brave New World*
> *worms in the rose*   *Lee 162*

the party's hostess
> some new drug in the basement
> crying like a child

CIA personnel
> helping local chemists
> set up LSD labs

in the Bay Area
> to monitor events   *Lee 188-89*
> STP Serenity

from Dow Chemical
> and the Edgewood Arsenal
> *like being shot out of a gun*   *Lee 187*

men with their Sunday morning
              rifle range target practice
       Black Panthers Ku Klux Klan

women who shyly hinted
              at ineffable orgies
       of acid nakedness

Ed Sanders the Fugs
              investigative poetics
       Out demons out

with *no respect whatsoever
              for the unassailable logic
       of the next step*   *Mailer 86*

two hundred pounds of daisies
              from Peggy Hitchcock
       to skybomb the Pentagon

Fort Funston Beach
              the Barb's first nude-in
       under the fixed gaze of the mounted police

dunes of iceplant and callas
              linnets in the sun and mist
       (To shoot a policeman

is a sacred act)   *Lee 265*
              the women in seaweed and surf
       wading as if to be washed

as clean as seals

IV.iii

There must be two of me
        I remember the surge
    of almost too vivid pleasure

when the sheriffs lined up
        their faces and numbers masked
    the streetlights' reflections

caught in the burnish
        of their identical helmets
    and we found we could hold our terrain

the smoking canisters
        of tear gas hurled back
    there were so many more of us

or to watch the incompetent
        Vice-President of Buildings
    who had never once met

anyone who could explain
        why his blueprints for Peoples' Park
    were denounced as murderous

he being as determined
        to maintain what he called order
    as the tribes to upheave it

the difference not always clear
        and when the helicopter
    darkened half the sky

with CS gas
        I myself wanted to reach
    for a machine-gun but

when the clenched fists went off
            down Telegraph towards
        the waiting fence

the canisters popping
            like white fourth of July rockets
        and the sheriffs loading their rifles

with .303 buckshot
            the moment everyone had been waiting for
        for someone James Rector to get killed

I watched from the second-story window
            of Wheeler Hall with John
        the middle-aged mafia contractor

boyfriend of my teaching assistant
            who had told her
        the night Bobby Kennedy was shot

our boys must have done it
            and whom the U.S. Government
        had flown to Saigon

to handle the waterfront corruption
            Through the thick glass and
        oak frame of the dormer window

we watched the meridional blue sky
            with so much white gas in it
        above the plane trees

which later sickened
            and wept their leaves
        and I said to him *John*

which was not his name *don't worry*
            I'm sure Karen is in the library
        she wouldn't be out there

and never said until this sentence
        the whiteness
    of those distraught mafia knuckles

is what I
        still carry with me
    from this supposedly historic day

IV.iv

When after the dinners
        in the expensive East Side restaurants
    I used to go back

to the Mission code machines
        speeding my dictated reports
    to Ottawa that night

with copies to Washington
        London Paris for possible
    sharing with *our* NATO *allies*

not a word I wrote then
        was worth being recorded
    let alone labeled TOP SECRET

Later reading declassified
        copies of the U.S. traffic
    of those years

I felt outside the dimensions
        of the flattened bureaucratese
    that once seemed normal

COMMIES KORCOMS CHICOMS   *Korean, Chinese Communists*
        from people in the State Department
    not really witting of course

but anxious to prove
        they were on the team
    if we are prepared abandon

hope influencing Sukarno
        and if we still believe army
    best bet to keep INDO

out of COMMIE *hands* etc.
        if we can give them
    this kind of shot in arm

they might have more inclination act   *DD '75 120D 1/9/65*
        Or in the very month
    of *Time* Magazine's disclosure

the disposal of the corpses
        has created a serious sanitation problem
    small rivers and streams

have been literally clogged with bodies
        river transportation
    has at places been impeded   *Time 12/17/65*

emotion without judgment
        as if *pour encourager les autres*
    while the language of world order

is one of judgment
        at any cost
    uncontaminated by emotion

e.g. *military leaders' campaign*
        to destroy PKI
    is moving swiftly and smoothly

(an outgoing from George Ball
        the opponent of escalation
    and *devil's advocate* i.e. the one lone dove)

we may be confronted within weeks
    with situation we have hoped for
    i.e. a new government   DD '76 83G 12/16/65

or this incoming from the new Ambassador
    elimination continues apace
    party formally terminated

in fourteen provinces
    only eleven more to go!
    continuing massacre Bali

many headless bodies
    encountered on roads
    tourists well advised

to postpone pleasure trips
    to island of the gods   DD '76 84A 12/20/65
    A society which

declassifies its documents
    after it is too late
    to make any difference

will publish anything
    as did the *L.A. Times* —
    The Communist Party

attempted to seize power
    and subjected the country   L.A. Times 11/15/75
    to a national bloodbath   Chomsky 216

Or you Robert Shaplen
    writing from CIA sources
    for *The New Yorker*

They went to their deaths
          in white funeral robes
     with an astonishing passivity

as if admitting their guilt   Shaplen 123-24

                    IV.v

Action! I do not mean
          the log bouncing four times
     down from the jackladder

into the Rivière aux Outardes
          the fluke by which I survived
     the stinking bunkhouse

of the Quebec North Shore Paper Company
          with men who could spend
     six weeks salary on a Rimouski weekend

even less the compromise
          Canadian amendment
     which to the distress of the French

passed by a large majority
          at the Conference on Diplomatic Intercourse
     in the grand hall of the Vienna Hofburg

I mean the melancholy beauty
          of a fog-calm morning
     on the Sproul Hall steps

which Governor Reagan
          had declared off-limits
     to any assembly

between a few chilly spectators
            and the gas-masked
       riot-helmeted highway patrol

we were thirty faculty
            asserting a high view
       of our constitutional rights

and when the patrolmen
            arms linked billy-clubs
       presented but not menacing

began to push us
            so silently you could still hear
       the baffled pigeons

the fountain in the wet gloom
            they came first to myself
       and to David Krech

who had already suffered
            his first bad heart attack
       I looked in his face

forgetting all the others
            as if to say *Krech*
       what does one do now

they are moving so slowly
            that if we somehow
       refuse to be displaced

we will have converted
            history into that moment
       of resolution

all of us have been waiting
            so many years for
       but it was too late

already we were
          being nudged to one side
     in slow motion

the way a sure hand guides
          crumbs off a table
     to where the captain

in the presence of all of us
          said *congratulations*
     for a job well done

but we all knew there
          is no easier task
     than to sweep away faculty

it was not in the next day's paper
          not even the campus paper
     and I knew afterwards

the failure was not just
          our lack of planned options
     but my much older habit

of inevitably looking
          to someone else
     and though Krech is now

dead I still think of
          that moment face turned
     impending sticks helmets

those baffled eyes

IV.vi

He who sits mind brooding
          over his self-restraint
          is called a hypocrite said Krishna   Bhag. Gita 3.6

or as Mailer observed
          at the steps of the Pentagon
          it was *a large blemish*

that they were supine
          like a string of fish   Mailer 276-77
          the left calling Martin Luther

King an Uncle Tom
          but Sir Winston Churchill
          found it *alarming*

and also nauseating to see
          the Viceroy summon
          a seditious Middle Temple lawyer

now posing as a fakir
          of a type well-known in the East
          striding half-naked up the steps

of the Viceregal palace   Payne 404
          Gandhi first met the Gita
          in the Sir Edwin Arnold translation

through the London Vegetarian Society
          and Madame Blavatsky's theosophists
          but what to Churchill seemed inauthentic

and to Indians unscholarly
          the Pandavas had exhausted all avenues
          the war was actually forced on them

it would be unbecoming of Arjuna
        as a hero and ksatriya   *warrior*
    to refuse to fight   *Betai 239, 237*

is just what makes Gandhi
        more than his roots
        as when for his acceptance

of voluntary fingerprinting
        he was felled *he Rama* with a cudgel   *O God*
        kicked and beaten in his blood

by a Pathan Mir Alam   *Payne 181*
        who would later apologize
    with a warm handclasp   *Erikson 204*

at the Hamidia mosque
        as the Johannesberg Indians
        burned their registration certificates

and he sustained himself in jail
        on Thoreau a life of Garibaldi
        and the Koran

and when he translated
        Ruskin's *Unto This Last*
        into his native Gujarati

it was as a text
        for Tolstoy Farm in the Transvaal
        and later the Sabarmati ashram

the first *fasting for light*   *Payne 441*
        was to force not the British
        but the leaders of the Depressed Classes

to rescind their demands
        for a separate electorate
    I would far rather

that Hinduism died
      than that untouchability lived   *Payne 439*
   and the last was to force

the new Indian cabinet
      to reverse itself
   and pay the new state of Pakistan

its share of the old divided treasury
      shunning the London Conference
   he trekked through the Muslim

villages of Noakhali
      where thousands of Hindus
   had been killed or forcibly converted

to hold prayer meetings
      once even in a mosque
   and gradually restore peace

Gandhi wrote to a friend
      truth and nonviolence have sustained me
   for the last sixty years

but today I seem to miss
      the certainty of that power   *Kytle 173*
   and when he was *he Rama* murdered   *O God*

the new government
      needing to honor him
   gave him a military funeral

transported his body
      on a flower-bedecked
   weapons carrier

while overhead Dakotas
        of the Royal Indian Air Force
    dipped in salute

with *showers of scented blossoms*   *Kytle 182*

                    IV.vii

On the night train to Kraków
        the Polish engineers
    among the ficelles of vegetables

and the smell of the peasants' tobacco
        would talk excitedly
    about the prospects for extracting sulphur

from great depths or the problem
        of feeding the cities now that
    the peasants had taken back

their family half-hectare plots
        (here they lowered their voices)
    and would not buy tractors

believing like ourselves
        in the *philosophy of growth*
    with its propensity to distance

the planners ever more from the people
        the barefoot goat-herd girl near Warsaw
    in the Breughel landscape

we beheld from the Vistula dike
        from the Leninist auto-critique
    published in Prague

suicidal leftist policies
          the Chinese comrades
     not averse to capitalizing   Mrázek 164-65

to which the Czech student
          of Professor Anderson
     added *No American*

could claim that U.S. training
          had strengthened Suharto   Mrázek 172
     who *tried to unify*

under the spirit of jago-satria   *fighting-cock, warrior*
          and was spared by the commandos
     because he was *not corrupted*

and *westernized*   Mrázek 184, 171
          It has been said many times
     but only by the powerless

wherever the quality of work
          is a function of productivity
     and not vice versa

(I will say it again)
          the growth of society
     towards maximized product

is accompanied by the enslavement of the subject

IV.viii

Clifford Geertz having just
          reread your *Notes*
     on the Balinese cockfight

how you were first accepted
        by the cautious villagers
    after you all fled

from the Javanese constabulary
        and how slaughter
    in the cock ring itself

after *red pepper*
        is stuffed down their beaks
    and up their anuses   Geertz '73 419

joins *pride to selfhood*
        selfhood to cocks
    and cocks to destruction   Geertz '73 444

a blood sacrifice
        offered to the demons
    to pacify their cannibal hunger   Geertz '73 420

depicting how things are among men
        not literally but almost worse
    imaginatively

what it says is
        it is of these emotions
    that society is built   Geertz '73 449

and of the combat
        between the terrible witch Rangda
    her eyes bulging like boils

and the endearing monster Barong
        a clash between the malignant
    and the ridiculous   Geertz '73 114

It is not your belief that men
        every last one of them are cultural artifacts   Geertz '73 51
    that I now question

or even that *the imposition*
　　　　of meaning on life
　　　　is the major end of human existence　　　　　　　*Geertz '73 434*

that Virgilian flourish
　　　　in your footnote to Max Weber
　　　　but your recurring interpretations

of the Balinese massacre
　　　　after what you choose to call
　　　　the bungled coup and its savage aftermath　　　　*Geertz '73 322*

My complaint is not
　　　　of your early field project
　　　　for Ford and the CIA-funded

Center at MIT
　　　　in which you preceded Pauker
　　　　or your commissioned study

on which local elites
　　　　would best play a role
　　　　in Rostow's *pre-take-off period*　　　　　　　　　*Geertz '63 3*

I will not cast that stone
　　　　from this front window
　　　　of the world's largest weapons lab

you who know about
　　　　puputan and *Tjalonarang*　　　　*ritual suicide, trance drama*
　　　　have the right to recall

the fact of *the massacre*
　　　　through the medium of the *cockfight*
　　　　the theatricality of trance　　　　　　　　　　　*Geertz '73 452*

but why did you write
　　　　several hundred thousand
　　　　people were massacred

largely villagers by other villagers
though there were some
army executions as well   *Geertz '73 282*

when even Shaplen admits
the murders in Bali
did not start until early December   *Shaplen 124*

that is until after
Colonel Edhie's commandos
with unit-names like *Dracula*

had finished in East Java   *P.D. Scott '85A 244*
the army began it
then handed the job over to the Balinese   *Shaplen 125*

that is to the *special teams*
set up under Nasution's
and Suharto's orders   *May 123*

and finally stopped the bloodletting
as the smell of burning houses
overpowered the customary

fragrance of the rich island flora   *Shaplen 125*
Clifford Geertz sometimes
the world is not as mysterious

as you and I might wish
why can you not write
as straightforwardly as *Time*   *Time 12/17/65*

about the land to which you returned
on a junta visa
and how can you write

about *the integrative revolution*
in a book that is indexed
to sixty-one countries

Paraguay the Soviet Union
but not the United States?

IV. ix

When some toys from the West
            were stolen out of the back seat
      of our Peugeot in Saska Kępa

I went without thinking
            to the Warsaw police
      A moustached officer

wrote down everything
            I had to say
      which was very little

and then asked me
            Was the door locked?
      I said I had no idea

probably not and he said
            Proszę Pana excuse me
      but it would be good in future

to keep your doors locked
            Our children are not used
      to seeing toys from the west

and you do not want
            to encourage them in crime
      those Sunday walks with

Cassie in her blue pram
            the well-dressed housewives
      offering in illegal dollars

twice what we had paid for it
        I told the officer
    I was withdrawing my complaint

He smiled and began to talk
        about his life as a policeman
    how much easier it had been

after Stalin had died
        In those days no one
    wanted to talk to us

even our own children
        sometimes mistrusting us
    despite what they learned at school

We talked for two hours
        and I think of him often
    as I read in the papers

of Solidarność suppressed
        how those must be
    privileged moments

one can so transcend history
        how today he would not dare
    to have such a conversation

nor I have the heart
        And yet those two hours
    in that ill-furnished precinct

seem somehow more true
        than the street battles since
    My own life is easier

no longer having to be consul
        I suspect that on our side
    officials of U.S. Steel

would find life easier
            not having to worry
        about what their children

were learning at university
            if they knew their smokestacks
        in Gary Indiana

did not threaten to kill off
            the salmon of Labrador
        and silence the weird laughter

of the loons

IV.x

The first coup
            after the fall of Kennedy and Minh
        was in Brazil

the highways pushed into the jungle
            big money
        for men like Daniel Ludwig

with CIA connections
            and the end of the Kaingang tribe
        feuds spread cleaving the society

wrote Jules Henry
            When Yakva says to me
        My cousin wants to kill me

I know he wants to kill his cousin
            who slaughtered his pigs
        for rooting up his corn   Girard 52, 54

but since then we have seen
          the corpses at Jonestown
   professors developing

subtle technologies
          for repression of protest
   and acceleration of the race

to nuclear suicide
          making Dan ask
   are we not Jonestown?

And what if the choices
          in Java were just
   as simple — to become

a technological graveyard
          stomachs torn open
   corpses deliberately impaled

on bamboo stakes   *Kartawidjaja 44*
          or a Malthusian one
   rice production beginning

to give way to high-yield
          low-nutrition cassava
   till petty landlords

rid themselves of peasants
          who had taken over the fields
   to enforce the government's

ineffectual land reform   *Shaplen 121*
          No! despite such choices
   it is clear we must resist

the black-shirted gangs
          some of whose own members
   experienced *recurring nightmares*

in which their victims appeared
        before them like Banquo's ghost
    and sought solace from doctors   *May 125*

like Wordsworth *enflamed with hope*
        at the square of the Carousel
    a *few weeks back*

heaped up with dead and dying
        until he seemed to hear
    a ghost *that cried to the*

whole city Sleep no more   *Prelude* 10.38-77
        and those deaths Pauker imagined
    no mere guilty memories

but portents

IV.xi

There is drought in the west
        I have just flown east for a weekend
    swum at my father's camp

and now dry myself in the
        mist among the wet
    red and yellow maple leaves

the lake so full the
        beach is flooded and we
    have to drop an anchor

from the boat's stern
        but the big news
    dividing the whole village

even my father from my mother
            is the Arab Gabr
        married to a Saudi princess

who wants to build
            an electronics factory
        on the other side of the lake

to train planeloads of Saudis
            brought over from Riyadh
        My father tells me

he can hardly afford the boat
            since the Arab bought up both marinas
        Ride's boathouse is

an office building with
            moslem arches in front
        my mother tells me

the French-Canadian shopkeepers
            need more business
        especially in winter

he wants to build here
            because he loves the lake so much
        there is no water in Arabia

Arbitrage! to save the dollar
            by monetizing oil   *Naylor 48-50*
        arms sales to the Shah

and I thought of Adnan Khashoggi
            the Indonesian shipping magnate
        Saudi friend of Pak

Chung Hee and Roy Furmark
            $106 million
        in Lockheed commissions

to Khashoggi alone   *Sampson '77 275*
          and twice that
     amount withdrawn by Khashoggi

from Rebozo's bank in Key Biscayne
          in May and November '72   *Adler 93*
     and of Lim Suharto's *cukong*   *Chinese partner*

who has bought the Hibernia bank
          with a branch on the Berkeley campus
     from profits on arms deals

handled by the finance
          manager of the McGovern campaign   *May 224-27*
     some kind of storm brewing

And I thought of the Arab in Wordsworth's dream
          a loud prophetic
          blast of harmony   *Prelude 5.96*

portending deluge

                    IV. xii

Is this not a lesson for you
          designers of policy
     who have been carefully trained

to ignore your instincts
          except that of surpassing
     You would not be so foolish

as to seek health through weight
          yet having sought growth
     through economic expansion

                    128

you now seek security
         through aggrandisement
      not even for commerce

at which others now exceed us
         but for the enforcement
      of miserable debt

Only our belief in strength
         could have made us so vulnerable
      only by patrolling the world

could we have become so hated
         only by fighting so hard
      to preserve the dollar

could we have driven gold
         to ten times its value
      in eleven years

as for those of us
         who are lucky enough
      not to sit hypnotized

our hands on the steering wheel
         which seems to have detached itself
      from the speeding vehicle

it is our job to say
         relax trust
      spend more time with your children

things can only go
         a little better
      if you do not hang on so hard

O Yava-dvipa   यवद्वीप
      in the Ramayana
adorned by seven kingdoms

thronged by gold mines   *Ramayana 4.40.30*
      Iabadiou for Ptolemaeus   Ἰαβαδίου
an island most fertile

and producing much gold   *Ptolemy 7.2.29*
      O Yeh P'o T'i   耶婆堤
      of the pilgrim Fa Hsien   *Fa Hsien 40; Sarkar 3*

in this country
      heretics and Brahmans flourish   *Beal 168*
      you have believed so often

in adjustment and Nirvana
      the annihilation of the self
Shiva Sogata rishi   *Sarkar 25*

Shiva and Buddha are one
      in Erlangga's stone inscription
      but different too

Sukarno's Nasakom
      Marxism and God
blended and blended and blended

to cultivate harmony
      a meeting place
      of all ideologies   *Legge 340-1*

even the PKI   *Indonesian Communist Party*
      looking to warrior heroes
      like Amir Machmud

once a PKI cardholder
        now chairman of the DPR   *Parliament*
   who arrested Subandrio

the first man I ever met
        at a cocktail party
   to be sentenced to death

(as for calling Amir Machmud
        a CIA agent
   where does it lead?)   TAPOL *3/86 9*

Yet even Sukarno
        who professed anger
   To hell with your aid

had authorized contracts
        allowing Stanvac and Caltex
   to increase their payments

arranged by a former
        OSS petroleum chief
   and Mobil adviser   *P.D. Scott '75 224*

directly to the accounts
        of Ibnu Sutowo's Permina   *P.D. Scott '85A 254*
   which played a key part

in bankrolling the coup
        according to *Fortune*   *Fortune 7/73 154*
   the army has never forgotten it   *P.D. Scott '75 258*

and which later hired
        the U.S. MILTAG chief
   as Washington lobbyist   *P.D. Scott '85A 255*

and though I used to believe
        Stanvac and Caltex were one
   total programmatic continuity

never the slightest deviation   *P.D. Scott '74 98-9*
        men from Stanvac and Caltex and Chase
    making OSS contacts

with Ho Chi Minh   *P.D. Scott '75 226*
        Devadeva Mahadeva   *God of Gods, Great God; Sarkar 35*
    I see now human faces

inwardly consumed
        Texaco the meanest
    and least self-deceiving   *Sampson '76 235-36*

unlike Mobil which
        with only ten percent of Aramco
    consistently wanted more oil   *Sampson '76 204*

hired William Henderson
        old American Friend of Vietnam
    we must be prepared to fight

for Southeast Asia   *P.D. Scott '74 127*
        and Kenneth Todd Young
    to alert Washington

to Vietnam's *crisis of confidence*   *P.D. Scott '74 128*
        Schumpeterian gates
    opening to opportunities

of creative destruction
        the writing of Tryksara
    $A + U + M$

on the surface of water   *Sarkar 66*

IV. xiv

He got off the bus and
            strode quickly down the levee
        to an uninhabited area

thirty-five feet below
            called Trinity River bottom
        where he practiced

with his second-hand Mannlicher-Carcano   *McMillan 279*
        wrote Priscilla Johnson
    not bothering to explain

that the man tracing the route
        was not Lee Harvey Oswald
    but a baffled FBI agent

almost a year later   *26 WH 61*
        checking out the fourth version
    of Marina's story

as coached by the office-mate
        of Jack Ruby's former attorney
    a senior FBI informant

whose meeting with Ruby
        on November 20
    was suppressed by the Warren Commission

and whose partner had been the conduit
        for payoffs from the mob   *P.D. Scott '76 36-37*
    do you understand what I'm saying?

but before I had finished
        the first third of this sentence
    the telephone had been disconnected

no less than four times
        just like six months before
      with the directors of The Fifth Estate

phone call after phone call
        as we hunted in vain
      for the trip words *army intelligence*

Alcohol Tobacco and Firearms Bureau
        or maybe just plain *rifle*
      and the time when Paul's voice

though just ten blocks away
        was like a phone call from Minsk
      I said *give us our sound back please*

and the burst of volume
        sent my ear reeling
      Even the lawyer

for the House Select Committee
        said *I've never heard*
      noises like that on a telephone before

and he never phoned back
        so I can't blame you Gore
      that after the fourth disconnection

I never got the chance
        to proceed with my sentence
      It was Bob Silvers

who explained two days later
        Gore asked me to try from New York
      and the operator said your extension

was not currently in service
        Gore has had time to reflect
      and has decided

to devote all his energy
        to gay political rights
    I can't blame you Gore

or the bleary-eyed hippie
        who followed me up Telegraph
    into four or five bookstores

and then back again (until
        I shook him through a second exit)
    saying over and over

we know who you are
        I work with the FBI
    sooner or later we are going to get you

and I could do nothing about it
        the poor guy
    was so obviously spacy

I can't blame anyone
        except maybe the advice
    to Odysseus from the blind man

for if a sentence
is left dangling in the mind too long

                IV.xv

But when you control
        most of the world
    you cannot stop

it has been managed before
        so you are expected
    to manage it again

the cunning plan
            becomes in the streets of Santiago
      a biblical whirlwind

Jakarta is coming
            in *Tribuna* a photograph
      of General Baeza

who led the assault
            on the presidential palace
      when they machine-gunned Allende

holding up in his hand
            the justifying card
      Djakarta se acerca   *Jakarta is approaching*
                                                              Freed 103-18

mailed to military officers
            to make them believe
      they were scheduled to be liquidated   *P.D. Scott '85A 259*

just as officers in Jakarta
            had been made to believe
      they were scheduled to be liquidated

after the CIA
            in Santiago was instructed
      to *author conclusive evidence*

Allende government
            planned to take country by force
      while the same card

Djakarta se acerca
            had been mailed to leftists
      and published in *El Siglo*

the aim the CIA
            had explained in '61
      was to polarize Laos   *Time 3/17/61*

136

where Hecksher had been Station Chief
            before presiding in Santiago
        over the so-called *abduction*

of the constitutionalist General Schneider
            and so three years later
        Z

the alleged secret plan
            to murder the chiefs
        of the armed forces

and the formal excuse for the coup   *Freed 117*
            Jakarta Jakarta
        there was no truth wrote David Phillips

to the belief of Mrs. Allende
            whom I know to be a fine person
        that CIA *was behind the coup*   *Phillips 250*

but when we talked
            before the Susskind show
        your right eye twitching

in its efforts to disrupt
            your attempt at a guiltless
        television smile

I could still not bring myself
            to be its accomplice and proclaim
        you murderer liar or even

Chief of WH Division   *Western Hemisphere*
            when CIA *agents*
        in Santiago assisted

in drafting bogus Z-plan
            documents alleging
        that Allende and his supporters

were planning to behead
          Chilean military commanders   *Szulc 724*
     and delle Chiaie's Aginter contacts

appear to have been active   .   *Laurent 163*
          in the bombings and riots
     of *Patria y Libertad*

supported by Kissinger
          and the 40 Committee   *Dinges 41, 54*
     Djakarta se acerca

before *P y L*
          joined with the military
     in the mop-up brigades

many of whose
          maybe 30,000 victims
     were *tortured to death*

the bodies sometimes
          disfigured beyond recognition   *Amn.Int. 253*
     headless corpses like logs

clogging the Nuble River   *Freed 110*

IV.xvi

For so long
          I have been sitting at my desk
     and I tremble

in front of the terrible blank paper
          the future from which it gathers words
     as the empire

gathers with métèque legions
        around the republic
    to displace its coinage

the earth stirs
        the skies have been opened
    the words must be terrible enough

I have sat on the crag
        above the Rad Lab
    accipiens sonitum

saxi de vertice pastor   *Aen.* 2.307–08
        where it is not hard
    to see the city flattened

after the fires of night
        the only movement
    billowing smoke and dust   *Aen.* 2.609

no people their flesh shall
        consume away
    while they stand upon their feet —   *Zech.* 14.12

this is no more
        than what the record tells us
    Eniwetok the atoll gone

the sky of a thousand suns
        all at once risen   *Bhag. Gita* 11.12
    the fearful mouths

between whose teeth are seen
        the warriors mangled   *Bhag. Gita* 11.17
    writhing without a word

and it is time to go

IV.xvii

And now East Timor
          where in 1977
     the Indonesian minister admits

perhaps 80,000 might have been killed   *Chomsky 175*
          that is to say one person out of eight
     by his own government's paracommandos

these gentle midnight faces
          the beetles which crowd their eyes
     From 1975 to 1977

the *New York Times* index
          entries for East Timor
     dropped from six columns

to five lines

IV.xviii

And it is easy
          to be introduced
     to Jacques' wife from New York

at Eloise's candlelight
          dinner party and
     say with complete decorum

not like with Gregor *Yes*
          your father was OSS
     Sullivan and Cromwell

and then Standard Oil
          your grandfather
     practiced law with the

son-in-law of J.P. Morgan
              and your cousin here I get
         two completely different

families confused but *in vino*
              and error I tell truth
         was secretary of the CIA's

Fairfield Foundation
              and his wife's cousin
         Christopher Emmet a descendant

of John Jacob Astor
              and President of the
         American Friends of Vietnam

was the one who accepted
              the tax-deductible donations   *Faenza 297*
         from the Brook Club to deliver   *P.D. Scott '72 193*

the Marseille waterfront
              into the hands of friendly
         socialists and behind them

the Corsican Guerinis
              already smuggling Saigon opium
         through the Armenians in Beirut

to be sold on Harlem streetcorners
              but why tell you this
         who married a French-Canadian

lawyer from Westmount
              and are serious about the piano
         now it is the new blood

from the Reagan entourage
              who meet with the Aginter
         veterans of the Guatemala bloodbath   *Kruger 21*

and no one in your
        generation seems to have preserved
    that ancient appetite for power

As long as I haven't
        offended you let
    us step out on the lawn

sloping down to where the
        streetlight in the maples
    at the edge of the water

shines on the long-disused
        lakefront bandstand
    where as a twelve-year-old

I was given popcorn
        to sit still as the
    Voltigeurs de Sherbrooke

went through their precarious
        Saturday-night arousals
    of John Philip Sousa's

martial nostalgia
        What is that whirr
    of low wings in the darkness

of the ornamental pine?
It is the owl

V.i

The village gathers
        for the shadow play
    the Mahabharata or in Kawi

the Barata Yudda
        the Great War
    in which the good Pendawas

return from the forest
        of solitude strong again
    to oust their evil cousins

in a battle so fierce
        the rivers stand still
    the sun pales

and the mountains tremble   *Covarrubias 241*
        just as Oppenheimer
    thought of Vishnu

the sky of a thousand suns   *Bhag. Gita* 11.12
        in the eclipsed shadows
    of Alamogordo

as a man of power
        drawn to the interpolated
    message of Krishna

on the flaming chariot
        standing between the lines
    the eve of the Brahma night   *Bhag. Gita* 8.17

which the *wajang koelit*   *shadow play*
        through centuries of alien
    occupation (the Portuguese

knowing only the word *rapio*)   *May 12*
        makes no mention of
    that the true sage

for whom light is darkness
        will learn from *ahimsa*
    to kill with detachment

to avoid the lawlessness
        leading to corrupted
    family women   *Betai 233-35*

and from this in turn
        to *varnasamkarah*
    intermixture of caste   *Bhag. Gita* 1.40

according to the Gita
        which Gandhi called his *mother*   *Betai i*
    and Dan *Eichman's bible*

(like Joshua's
        Sun stand thou still
    while the Israelis

avenged themselves upon their enemies
        till they were consumed
    that the rest of them

entered fenced cities
        for thus shall the Lord do)   *Joshua* 10.12-25
    first warriors then clowns

the mocking of masters with respect
       the word *act*
      a mountain burning with fire

and the day shone not   *Rev. 8.8,12*
       the forests are dying
       I think of my friend Dan

once first across the paddies
       to hurl his grenade
       into the machine-gun nest

or coming out of the Saigon
       restaurant in black tie
       after leaving Germaine   *'73 Hearings 3886*

saw Michel with a pistol
       reached down and
       scooped sand into his eyes

having already learned
       there were friends for whom he would die
       and no greater glory

vengeance compassion   *Iliad 24.503; Aen. 12.932*
       and then detachment
       (detachment not from care

but from the past)
       when he and Allen and the others
       lined up on the railway tracks

at Rocky Flat
       the nuclear warheads plant
       object or subject

you are free to call this
       either witness or theatre
       it was by all means play

and in the final seconds
the train stopped

V. ii

If you bring forth
        what is within you
    it will save you

if you do not bring forth
        what is within you
    it will destroy you   *Gospel of Thomas 45.29-33; Pagels 152*

the papyrus
        removed after two millennia
    from its red jar

and dumped on the straw
        next to the avenger's oven
    by chance not

among those his mother burned
        I read the gnostic
    Gospel of Thomas

and see belatedly
        it was unavoidable
    the saving nausea

the wind-driven angel
        in the all-night tempest
    the blue sea shining

behind the white bones
        of the affable skeleton
    on the painted altarpiece

Morieris et non vives   *You will die and not live*
          in the mountain chapel
          above Lake Como

this smile from my past
          still comes to me
          not those of the scholars

rattling their teacups
          back in the Villa Serbelloni
          alone we go mad

and yet to be human
          is to have this sense
          we are unfit for the crowded maze

and if for a moment
          I am too calm
          at the napalm which descends

on yet another nation
          Steve Carr dead in Van Nuys   *McMichael 7*
          the message for Jack Terrell

you'll be shot
          if you step off that plane
          not my own

inconsiderable death threats
          but that clean morning in Palo Alto
          the former Green Beret

who just the night before
          had said he would talk to us
          about opium in Laos

showing us the sharp black hole
          in his M.G.'s red steel door
          the floorboards hardly scorched

and saying *that hot*
       an imploded thermal charge
     must have come from my old unit

and if from such terror
       we each acknowledge
     we are not normal

in this world where
       we live by forgetting
     as the storm lets up

the white snowflakes dance
       around the streetlamp
     and the flared ghost

once *fleet-footed pursuing*   *Iliad* 9.505, 512
       down the black oak
     still our familiar and yet

if you bring forth
what is within you

                V.iii

Where no vision is
       the people die and yet   *Prov. 29.18*
     it is by imagination's failure

that we go on surviving
       reasonable by day
     and then by night

the nightmare
       where Bisson and Chevalier were ousted
     and they multiply bombs

more than 1200
        nuclear explosions
    since the Jornada del Muerto

and not since the first
        have there been physicists
    who renounced their clearance

shall I say once again
        why there will be more war
    small and great alike

all are given to gain
        prophet and priest practice fraud   Jer. 6.13
    and the people love it   Jer. 5.31

yet if we return
        to the old ways
    of the ashvattha tree   Bhag. Gita 15.1

fallen fruit in the snow
        small ghost fading in the dawn
    it must be to recognize

not to re-enter
        the fierce gates of the past
    for when the blind woman has seen

the terrible beauty
        of energy come forth
    to destroy the worlds   Bhag. Gita 11.32

O Apollo lord of
        the light you blind me   Agamemnon 1227
    we cannot like children

go back to duty and *svadharma*   *special or caste duty*
        let there be the courage
    not just to have seen

but to ease into the world
the unreal
breathing within us

SOURCES

Adler, Renata. "Searching for the Real Nixon Scandal." *Atlantic Monthly,* December 1976.

Amnesty International. *Report on Torture.* New York: Farrar, Strauss & Giroux, 1975.

AR: U.S. Congress. House. Select Committee on Assassinations. *Final Report.* Washington, D.C.: GPO, 1979.

Auerbach, Erich. *Literary Language and Its Public.* New York: Pantheon Books, 1965.

Baker, Ray Stannard. *American Chronicle.* New York: Scribner, 1945.

Bateson, Gregory, and Margaret Mead. *Balinese Character.* New York: New York Academy of Sciences, 1942.

Beal, Samuel. *Travels of Fah-Hsian and Sung-Kun, Buddhist Pilgrims, from China to India (400 A.D. and 518 A.D.).* London: Susil Gupta, 1934.

Becker, Elizabeth. *When the War Was Over.* New York: Simon and Schuster, 1986.

Belo, Jane. *Bali: Rangda and Barong.* New York: J. J. Augustin, 1949.

———. *Trance in Bali.* New York: Columbia University Press, 1960.

Berle, Adolf. *Navigating the Rapids.* New York: Harcourt Brace Jovanovich, 1973.

Berlin, Isaiah. *Personal Impressions.* Harmondsworth, Middlesex: Penguin, 1982.

Betai, Ramesh S. *Gita and Gandiji.* Ahmedabad: Gujarat Vidyapith, 1970.

Blum, John Morton. *From the Morgenthau Diaries: Years of Urgency 1938–1941.* Boston: Houghton Mifflin Co., 1965. Revised and condensed in *Roosevelt and Morgenthau.* Boston: Houghton Mifflin Co., 1970.

Brown, Anthony Cave. *The Last Hero: Wild Bill Donovan.* New York: Vintage Books, 1984.

Bulletin of Concerned Asian Scholars. Summer–Fall 1971.

Bullitt, Orville H., ed. *For the President: Personal and Secret.* Boston: Houghton Mifflin Co., 1972.

Chomsky, Noam, and Edward S. Herman. *The Washington Connection and Third World Fascism.* Boston: South End Press, 1979.

Church: See U.S. Congress. Senate. Select Committee to Study Governmental Operations with Respect to Intelligence Activities.

Council on Foreign Relations. *The War and Peace Studies of the Council on Foreign Relations, 1939–1945.* New York, 1946.

Covarrubias, Miguel. *Island of Bali.* New York: Alfred A. Knopf, 1942.

Crouch, Harold. *The Army and Politics in Indonesia.* Ithaca: Cornell University Press, 1978.

Curtius, Ernst Robert. *European Literature and the Latin Middle Ages.* New York: Harper, 1963.

Davies, W.H. *Autobiography of a Supertramp.* New York: Alfred A. Knopf, 1917.

DD: *Declassified Documents.* Carrollton Press.

Dinges, John, and Sol Landau. *Assassination on Embassy Row.* New York: Pantheon Books, 1980.

Djwa, Sandra. *The Politics of the Imagination: A Life of F.R. Scott.* Toronto: McClelland and Stewart, 1987.

Doyle, Kevin. "Prince Who Fell from Grace." *Atlas,* December 1976.

Dulles, John Foster. *War, Peace and Change.* New York: Harper and Brothers, 1939.

Duroselle, Jean-Baptiste. *From Wilson to Roosevelt.* New York: Harper and Row, 1968.

Erikson, Erik H. *Gandhi's Truth: On the Origins of Militant Nonviolence.* New York: W.W. Norton, 1969.

Faenza, Roberto, and Marco Fini. *Gli Americani in Italia.* Milan: Feltrinelli, 1976.

Fairbank, John. "Comment." *Bulletin of Concerned Asian Scholars.* Summer–Fall 1971.

Fifield, Russell H. *Southeast Asia in United States Policy.* New York: Frederick A. Praeger, for the Council on Foreign Relations, 1963.

Freed, Donald, with Fred Landis. *Death in Washington.* Westport, Conn.: Lawrence Hill, 1980.

Geertz, Clifford. *Peddlers and Princes.* Chicago: University of Chicago Press, 1963.

———. *The Interpretation of Cultures.* New York: Basic Books, 1973.

———. *Negara.* Princeton: Princeton University Press, 1980.

Girard, Rene. Translated by Patrick Gregory. *Violence and the Sacred.* Baltimore: Johns Hopkins Press, 1977.

Hamburger, Michael, and Christopher Middleton. *Modern German Poetry 1910–1960.* New York: Grove Press, 1960.

Hearings: See U.S. Congress.

Homans, George C. "Commentary on Schlesinger." *American Sociological Review,* February 1963. In *The Structure of Evil* by Ernest Becker. New York: The Free Press, 1968.

———. *The Human Group.* New York: Harcourt, Brace and World, 1950.

Hoopes, Townsend. *The Devil and John Foster Dulles.* Boston: Little, Brown, 1973.

Hougan, Jim. *Spooks.* New York: William Morrow, 1978.

Hudson, Michael. *Super Imperialism.* New York: Holt, Rinehart & Winston, 1972.

Ignatieff, George. *The Memoirs of George Ignatieff: The Making of a Peacemonger.* Toronto: University of Toronto Press, 1985.

Kaplan, Justin. *Lincoln Steffens: a Biography.* New York: Simon and Schuster, 1974.

Kartawidjaja [Pipit Rochijat]. Translated by Ben Anderson. "Am I PKI or Non-PKI?" *Indonesia,* October 1985.

Kolko, Gabriel. *The Politics of War: The World and United States Foreign Policy, 1943–1945.* New York: Random House, 1968.

Krause, Gregor. *Bali.* Munich: Georg Muller, 1926.

Kruger, Henrik. *The Great Heroin Coup.* Boston: South End Press, 1980.

Kwitny, Jonathan. *The Crimes of Patriots.* New York: W.W. Norton, 1987.

Kytle, Calvin. *Gandhi, Soldier of Nonviolence.* New York: Grosset and Dunlap, 1969.

Laurent, Frédéric. *L'Orchestre noir.* Paris: Stock, 1978.

Lee, Martin, and Bruce Shlain. *Acid Dreams: The CIA, LSD and the Sixties Rebellion.* New York: Grove Press, 1985.

Legge, J. D. *Sukarno: A Political Biography.* London: Allen Lane: The Penguin Press, 1972.

Lernoux, Penny. *In Banks We Trust.* Garden City, N.Y.: Anchor Press/Doubleday, 1984.

Lippmann, Walter. *The Phantom Public.* New York: Macmillan, 1930.

Mailer, Norman. *The Armies of the Night.* New York: New American Library, 1968.

Mandelstam, Nadezhda. *Hope Against Hope: A Memoir.* New York: Atheneum, 1979.

Marshall, Jonathan V. "Bankers and the Search for a Separate Peace During World War II." Master's thesis, Cornell University, 1981.

————, Peter Dale Scott, and Jane Hunter. *The Iran-Contra Connection*. Boston, South End Press, 1987.

May, Brian. *The Indonesian Tragedy*. London: Routledge and Kegan Paul, 1978.

[McMichael, David.] *Crime and the Contras—A Summary Report*. Washington: International Center for Development Policy, [1986].

McMillan, Priscilla Johnson. *Marina and Lee*. New York: Harper and Row, 1978.

Morton, Frederic. *The Rothschilds*. New York: Fawcett, n.d.

Mosley, Leonard. *Dulles*. New York: The Dial Press/James Wade, 1978.

Mrázek, Rudolf. *The United States and the Indonesian Military 1945–1965: A Study of an Intervention*. 2nd vol. Prague: Academia, 1978.

Naylor, R. T. *Hot Money and the Politics of Debt*. New York: Linden Press/Simon and Schuster, 1987.

Pagels, Elaine. *The Gnostic Gospels*. New York: Random House, 1979.

Pauker, Guy J. *Communist Prospects in Indonesia*. Santa Monica: RAND Corporation, RM-5753-PR, November 1964.

————. "The Role of the Military in Indonesia." In *The Role of the Military in Underdeveloped Countries,* edited by John J. Johnson. Princeton: Princeton University Press, 1962.

Payne, Robert. *The Life and Death of Mahatma Gandhi*. London: Bodley Head, 1969.

PP: *The Pentagon Papers: The Defense Department History of United States Decisionmaking on Vietnam*. Boston: Beacon Press, 1971.

Phillips, David Atlee. *The Night Watch*. New York: Atheneum, 1977.

Powers, Thomas. *The War at Home*. New York: Grossman, 1973.

Ransom, David. "Ford Country." In *The Trojan Horse,* edited by Steve Weissman. San Francisco: Ramparts Press, 1974.

Reid, Ed, and Ovid Demaris. *The Green Felt Jungle*. New York: Pocket Books, 1964.

Sampson, Anthony. *The Arms Bazaar*. New York: Viking, 1977.

————. *The Seven Sisters*. New York: Viking, 1975.

Sarkar, Himansu Bhusan. *Indian Influences on the Literature of Java and Bali*. Calcutta: Greater India Society, 1934.

Schurmann, Franz. *The Logic of World Power*. New York: Pantheon Books, 1974.

————, Peter Dale Scott, and Reginald Zelnik. *The Politics of Escalation in Vietnam.* New York: Fawcett, 1966.

Scott, F. R. *Collected Poems.* Toronto: McClelland and Stewart, 1981.

Scott, Frank R. *A New Endeavour: Selected Political Essays, Letters, and Addresses.* Edited by Michiel Horn. Toronto: University of Toronto Press, 1986.

Scott, Frederick George. *The Great War as I Saw It.* Vancouver: Clarke and Stuart, 1934.

Scott, Peter Dale. *Crime and Cover-Up: the CIA, the Mafia, and the Dallas-Watergate Connection.* Berkeley: Westworks, 1976.

————. "Exporting Military-Economic Development." In *Ten Years' Military Terror in Indonesia,* edited by Malcolm Caldwell. Nottingham: Spokesman Books, 1975.

————. "The United States and the Overthrow of Sukarno." *Pacific Affairs,* Summer 1985.

————. "De Verenigde Staten & Indonesie 1965." In *Indonesie: De Waarheid Omtrent 1965.* Amsterdam: Indonesia Media, 1985.

————. "The Vietnam War and the CIA-Financial Establishment." In *Remaking Asia: Essays on the American Uses of Power,* edited by Mark Seldon. New York: Pantheon Books, 1974.

————. *The War Conspiracy.* Indianapolis and New York: Bobbs Merrill, 1972.

Shaplen, Robert. *Time Out of Hand.* New York: Harper and Row, 1969.

Shoup, Lawrence H., and William Minter. *Imperial Brain Trust.* New York: Monthly Review Press, 1977.

Smith, R. Harris. *OSS.* Berkeley: University of California Press, 1972.

Smith, Walter Buckingham. *Economic Aspects of the Second Bank of the United States.* Cambridge: Harvard University Press, 1953.

Stock, Noel. *The Life of Ezra Pound.* San Francisco: North Point Press, 1982.

Szulc, Tad. *The Illusion of Peace.* New York: Viking, 1978.

U.S. Congress. House. Committee on Government Operations. *Oversight Hearings into the Operations of the IRS, Hearings.* Washington, D.C.: GPO, 1975.

————. Senate. Committee on Foreign Relations. *Multinational Corporations and United States Foreign Policy, Hearings,* Part XII. Washington, D.C.: GPO, 1976.

————. Senate. Committee on the Judiciary. *Institute of Pacific Rela-*

tions, Hearings. Washington, D.C.: GPO, 1952.

---. Senate. Select Committee to Study Governmental Operations with Respect to Intelligence Activities. *Foreign and Military Intelligence,* Report No. 94-755, Book I. Washington, D.C.: GPO, 1976.

---. Senate. Select Committee on Presidential Campaign Activities. *Presidential Campaign Activities of 1972: Senate Resolution 60, Hearings.* Washington, D.C.: GPO, 1973.

Van Dusen, Henry P. *The Spiritual Legacy of John Foster Dulles.* Philadelphia: Westminster Press, 1960.

WH: U.S., Warren Commission. *Hearings.* Washington, D.C.: GPO, 1964.

Wisely, William. *A Tool of Power: The Political History of Money.* New York: John Wiley and Sons, 1977.

de Zoete, Beryl and Walter Spies. *Dance and Drama in Bali.* Kuala Lumpur and London: Oxford University Press, 1973.

AUTHOR'S NOTE

Since I first wrote this poem in 1980, many more people have helped than I can name here. Chief among these have been my colleagues, students, and other friends at Berkeley, especially the group of poets who used to meet with the late Josephine Miles. For assistance in the poem's final stages I must especially thank Ellen Seligman, Bernice Eisenstein, Russell Brown, and James Schamus, and Vic Marks of the Typeworks.

In 1983 I read much of the poem to a Berkeley poetry workshop led by Robert Hass. A week later I received in the mail an extensive, anonymous critique of the poem, offering line-by-line appreciations and emendations. For six months I knew only that there existed someone who had puzzled out some of the poem's mechanics, better at times than I had myself.

Then by good fortune I encountered at a reception this unknown editor, Kim Maltman, and his close friend Roo Borson. The two, well-known Canadian poets, have continued over the years to sharpen my awareness of what this poem is up to, and even on occasion to present themselves as my Muse's attorneys. I have accepted enough of their many suggestions to make *Coming to Jakarta*, in a strangely rewarding way, no longer wholly my own.

(Because Kim is also a particle physicist, the poem, which ends with evocations of Oppenheimer's Hindu apocalypse, ironically received its final editing sessions amid minatory thunder and hailstorms in Los Alamos, the University of California weapons facility in New Mexico.)

I hope soon to finish revising this poem's sequel, *Listening to the Candle: A Poem on Impulse*, dedicated to my mother, Marian Dale Scott.

* * *

Portions of *Coming to Jakarta* have already appeared in *The Berkeley Graduate* (II.iv, II.xvii, IV.x), the *Berkeley Poetry Review* (I.ii), *Berkeley U.S.A.*, by Anne Moose (Berkeley, California: Alternative Press, 1981, II.iv), and the anthology *'What Thou Lovest Well Remains': 100 Years of Ezra Pound*, ed. Richard Ardinger (Boise, Idaho: Limberlost Press, 1986, II.v).

A PARTIAL CHRONOLOGY

1957   CIA approves direct aid to rebel Indonesian army colonels.

3/14/57   Partly in response to U.S.-subsidized regional dissension, Indonesian President Sukarno declares martial law.

5/18/58   CIA pilot shot down and captured in Sumatra.

8/1/58   U.S. begins upgraded program of military assistance to Indonesian Army as "encouragement" to carry out plan "for the control of Communism."

8/59   RAND Conference on "The Role of the Military in Underdeveloped Countries." Guy Pauker urges Indonesian Army to carry out "a control function."

1959–60   Council on Foreign Relations Study Group on Southeast Asia, followed in 1963 by Prof. Fifield's book.

3/22/61   CIA memo expresses frustration with pro-Sukarno record of Indonesian Army General Nasution.

12/18/63   Incoming President Johnson withholds economic aid to Indonesia.

1962–65   U.S. cuts back on military aid to Indonesia, except to selected anti-Sukarno elements of Army.

1965   1958 CIA rebel contact visits Washington, recommends Suharto as new leader for Indonesia.

5/65   Intelligence-controlled Lockheed payoffs to Indonesian influence-men redirected to Suharto's financial backer, General Alamsjah.

7/65   Secret contract to deliver U.S. planes for "civic action" to Indonesian Army.

9/65   Indonesian generals warned of impending assassination plots. Planted stories abroad speak of arms-smuggling to Java from mainland China.

9/30/65	Jani and his pro-Sukarno supporters on Army General Staff are rounded up and murdered. Nasution escapes.
10/1/65	Massacre of Communists and ethnic Chinese begins. Suharto takes over, closes all papers except Communist and one other on left.
10/2/65	Questioned issue of Communist paper supports alleged coup attempt of September 30; becomes pretext to continue massacre.
10–12/65	RPKAD Commandos of Col. Sarwo Edhie spread massacre to other parts of Indonesia. More than 500,000 killed.
3/11/66	Suharto arrests pro-Sukarno ministers in partial coup.
6/19/66	James Reston in *New York Times* describes "Indonesian massacre" as "A Gleam of Light in Asia."
3/13/67	Suharto announces that Sukarno is no longer President.
1967	Richard Nixon reportedly tells U.S. Ambassador to Indonesia that "Indonesian experience" shows how "we should handle our relationships on a wider basis . . . in the world."
1973	CIA agents in Chile help draft bogus documents alleging that Allende plans to behead military commanders. Small cards distributed with words *Djakarta se acerca* ("Jakarta is approaching").
1981	Former CIA agent Ralph McGehee reveals CIA deception operation for Indonesia in 1965, designed to set the stage for a massacre.

ABOUT THE AUTHOR

Peter Dale Scott was born in 1929 in Montreal, Canada. He studied at McGill University (B.A., 1949), the Institut D'Etudes Politiques, Paris (1950), and University College, Oxford (1950–52), before receiving his Ph.D. in Political Science from McGill in 1955. In 1953 he taught at Sedbergh School, Montebello, Quebec. In 1956 he married Maylie Marshall; they have three children. From 1957 to 1961 he was a Canadian diplomat, serving at the United Nations General Assembly, and for two years in Warsaw, Poland. Since 1961 he has taught at the University of California, Berkeley, where he is now a Professor of English. While at Berkeley he became involved in the anti-Vietnam War movement, as a result of which he has published books dealing with the Vietnam War and the assassination of John F. Kennedy: *The Politics of Escalation in Vietnam* (in collaboration); *The War Conspiracy; The Assassinations: Dallas and Beyond* (in collaboration); and *Crime and Cover-Up*. His most recent prose book is *The Iran-Contra Connection,* co-authored with Jonathan Marshall and Jane Hunter (Boston: South End Press, 1987 and Montreal: Black Rose Books, 1987). In the realm of poetry, he has published *Poems* (Oxford: Fantasy Press, 1952); *Rumors of No Law* (Austin, Tex.: Thorp Springs Press, 1980); *Prepositions of Jet Travel* (Berkeley: Berkeley Poetry Review, 1981); and *Heart's Field* (Berkeley: Aroca Press, 1986). His translations (with Czeslaw Milosz) of the Polish poet Zbigniew Herbert were first published in 1968 and recently reissued. *Coming to Jakarta* was completed while he was a visiting Senior Fellow at the International Center for Development Policy, Washington, D.C.